Why
I Am A
Democratic
Socialist
and
Not A
Tea Party
Republican
Capitalist

Edward G. Weiss, Ph.D.

This essay is an abridgement of a Doctoral Dissertation. It is bibliography and end-note free. I hope I have made your reading more enjoyable by omitting the academic economicese. If I have not, I apologize.. This essay is important to all of us and it is important that it be understood If you have any questions or wish to obtain source material, please e-mail me at eddiegTHOI@gmail.com. I will do my best to respond quickly.

Thank you to my dissertation committee, Dr. Harold T. Walsh, Dr. Winston A. Wilkinson, Dr. John P. Henderson and Dr. Charles P. Larrowe

ABOUT THE AUTHOR

Ed Weiss is a retired Professor of Economics and Business Ethics. He was responsible for the development of his University's MBA Program and one of the world's first on-line Business Administration Programs. He has taught at National-Louis University, Chicago, IL, Bethel College, N. Newton, KS, University of Maryland-University College in Europe, Valparaiso University, Valparaiso, IN and Michigan State University, East Lansing, MI. He was also a consultant for several small businesses. He is not and never has been a communist. Before his academic career, he had been a NASD Principal, as well as a Home Office Life Insurance Underwriter, then a Brokerage Field Underwriter. Currently, he resides in Mexico and has written and will soon publish four novels.

Further information including his full vita, can be obtained at https://eddieg.theblogpress.com/

Originally Titled
TOWARDS A BETTER UNDERSTANDING OF CAPITALISM
(Including End Notes and Bibliography)
Available through ProQuest
8603493

CONTENTS

INTRODUCTION

Capitalism is widespread. Some variation of it is present in most of the world. It is an important economic system and needs to be better understood, but it is not. Many speak and write about capitalism. It is often attacked, often defended. Since capitalism is as widespread an economic system as it is, we will benefit from a *better-than-usual* understanding of it. This essay will wade through the waters of propaganda and ideology to obtain that *better-than-usual* understanding of it so that it might be better judged.

If a society is to exist in a meaningful way, its members must share an ideology, common beliefs about how the affairs of the society should be conducted. A society often has a second set of values which alleges that it clarifies and justifies the core ideology, but frequently conflicts with it. For example, competition is a major tenet of the capitalist ideology, yet it seldom exists in fact. From an economic perspective, this tenet only tries to justify the current mode of property ownership and distribution of wealth and income.

Since many are mistaken or confused about what *capitalism* is and what it is intended to accomplish when claiming that it is the superior economic system, the reasons for their claim need to be listed and reviwed. To do this, it is necessary to critique the assumptions of the *standard* capitalist model. Then since all economic activity takes place in the real world, the political backdrop needs examination followed by a short course on economic systems analysis.

Several suggestions, if heeded, might help bring the practice of capitalism into line with its stated aims and ideology.

1   CAPITALISM

"Capitalism is one of those terms frequently used but seldom defined, and even less frequently understood. Exactly what does it mean?" Many people would like to know *exactly* what is meant by *capitalism* particularly when used by those who assert it to be *the* superior economic system.

Understanding this difficult to define term is even more difficult because it is one which is laden with ideology. The term is used by both its supporters and its attackers, and often, they don't mean the same or even similar things. Since each intends something different from that which is intended by the other, it is usually difficult to determine which meaning of capitalism is being used in any given instance. Even when the user's ideological position is known, it is still difficult to ascertain what is meant. Everyone seems to use the term differently. "Exactly what does it mean?"

One would think that a proponent of something would wish to be as clear as possible about what one is proposing. Unfortunately, this hoped-for clarity seldom exists where capitalism is concerned. Often, different advocates, even those who are basically on the same side of the ideological question, have different perspectives. This results in different proponents emphasizing or deemphasizing different aspects of capitalism.

This is usually because each has different self-interests to protect or to promote thus accounting for their different perspectives. Acting to protect or to promote one's self-interests should be expected. A basic tenet of capitalism is, after all, to act in this manner. But, different people acting to protect or to promote different self-interests makes it difficult to know what any particular supporter of capitalism means when that person uses the term *capitalism* unless one first knows what that person's self-interests are and what position that person is attempting to promote.

It is also difficult to know what the term means when it is used by detractors of capitalism because, like the system's advocates, those detractors come in many different varieties. Even when detractors are erudite, they usually use the term pejoratively and are not easy to follow because they also have ideologies and self-interests to promote, and like those of the system's advocates, their ideologies and self-interests often differ greatly from one another.

The term should be used in a more objective manner as opposed to the usual subjective one that is mostly encountered. Arriving at an objective definition of capitalism is not easy, but the attempt needs to be made.

Even so, it is unlikely that all will agree with whatever definition is lastly settled upon here. That this disagreement is probable helps make clear the difficulties faced when attempting to define capitalism. Adequately defining capitalism involves much more than just the straight forward act of defining. It also requires both perspective and judgment. One ingredient, perspective, hardly ever will be the same for many, let alone everyone.

You must be able to see for yourself why our final definition is what it is. If you think that it could be more objective or if you disagree for any other reason, at least you will be able to analyze the reasoning process used in arriving at it. This is more than can be said for most such definitions.

In the search for this definition of capitalism and the capitalist model, many mainstream economics texts, representing all levels of college and university instruction, were reviewed. None of them, irrespective of level, did anything other than to state their definition and present their assumptions. None presented any theoretical analyses though one would expect that they would.

Representative of most definitions is the following: Capitalism is "an economic system based on private ownership of productive resources and allocation of goods [and resources] according to the signals provided by the free markets."

Another says: "Capitalism is a system of economic organization characterized by private ownership of the factors of production and their operation for profit under predominantly competitive conditions." Another says, it is a "form of economic organization in which the means of production are privately owned and operated for profit and where freely operating markets coordinate the activities of consumers, businesses, and all suppliers of resources."

Others do not give a definition at all. They just present its philosophy. For instance, "Capitalism has many names. It's called the free enterprise system or the private enterprise system or the competitive free enterprise system or the laissez-faire system." Or, "The philosophy of capitalism is the philosophy of the market process, the philosophy of Adam Smith's laissez faire, of 'consumer sovereignty and the invisible hand.' It's the philosophy of individual freedom, of private property, of rewards for productivity. The idea is that if people and businesses are left free to make their own choices, everything will come out better for everybody." The claim that "everything will come out better for everybody" is an important one and needs to be defended.

The definitions cited above are taken from introductory texts, but even those texts used at the intermediate and graduate levels of instruction do not attempt to define the term. These authors seem take both a *standard* definition of capitalism and their readers' knowledge of it for granted.

Only one advanced text among those reviewed gives any attention at all to a definition of capitalism." Capitalism as a type of economic society is characterized by private ownership of the factors of production and by private initiative, guided by the profit motive, in the conduct of production." Though its definition is more sophisticated, it also merely puts forth the nature of capitalism without any analysis.

One text, an *Anti* text, says that the partial equilibrium model is but a "simplified version taught to many undergraduates [and is] obviously incomplete and inconsistent." Though true, most economists, including those in colleges and universities, believe and defend this "simplified version" *as is* . Perhaps, that is the reason for the inadequate analysis of the system's assumptions. The ones who should do it themselves believe too much in this "simplified version".

A better definition of capitalism that I have found is "an economic system oriented toward the accumulation of capital (or generalized, abstract wealth), coordinated by a market system in which land, labor and capital have become 'factors of production.'" It is better because it considers the greatest number of factors. It states the purpose of capitalism as well as what capitalism is and how the providers of the factors of production, particularly labor are viewed as commodities. They are things that are bought and sold.

All the definitions of capitalism given in these texts, except the last one, seem to be attempting to hide the real end of the system, the accumulation of great wealth and the power that results from the possession of that wealth. This is interesting because the reason most often given for adopting capitalism, or continuing with it if already adopted, is that "capitalism is the system that serves society best."

Milton Friedman is one of the few advocates of capitalism who admit the problems that accompany this concentration of wealth and power. He also appears to fear it. He correctly sees this accumulation as socially undesirable and in conflict with arguments given for the capitalist system. However, he mistakenly places the blame for the conditions that allow the accumulation of vast wealth on government interference with the market rather than on capitalism itself.

He uses the term *competitive capitalism* as opposed to just *capitalism*. He apparently does this because he sees a difficulty with the use of the unadorned word *capitalism* though he does not explicitly say so. This apparent difficulty arises for good reason. Capitalism as it exists is not competitive, and almost everyone agrees that competition is a condition which must exist if capitalism is to be an acceptable economic system. If it is not competitive, there will continue to be severe contradictions between its ideology and its reality. One or the other must be changed if the conflict is to be eliminated.

Neither does he define the ideology. As do many advocates of capitalism, he just assumes that everybody accepts the *standard* version.

The definition of capitalism that is emerging is the economic system in which private property, large and expensive capital equipment, and labor power, purchased from others, are used to produce goods and services. Labor is treated as a commodity, traded along with other factors of production in a free market, just like the consumer goods produced by those factors. Further, all production and trading strives to minimize costs of production, primarily labor which is usually the largest cost in the endeavor and to increase sales and the prices of those sales in their profit seeking ventures. That profit is then accumulated as an abundance of wealth and then used as additional capital in the production process. Luxury is no longer the end of possessing wealth. All this economic activity takes place under predominantly competitive conditions and without government interference.

The goal then is profit. What takes place under the capitalist mode of production would not take place if profit were not forthcoming. This is what Marx meant when he said that capitalism would not produce anything simply because it had value in use. It also would have to generate a profit.

Even though mainstream definitions of capitalism are incomplete and inaccurate, they still are given to students so that they will know what they are studying. But, they don't.

Another difficulty is that capitalism has undergone many transformations over the centuries. First, there was *mercantilist capitalism* accompanied by early *petite bourgeoisie capitalism*. "One can date the capitalist era as beginning in the sixteenth century. But, it requires hindsight, illuminated by an understanding of the later development of industrial capitalism."

Even so, when the capitalistic era actually began is not a well-settled point. People didn't then know that they were experiencing the birth of capitalism when it was actually happening. It wasn't until later, when capitalism was almost fully developed that we were able to look back and review its birth.

This early *mercantilist capitalism* was followed by the *manufacturing capitalism* of the Industrial Revolution. After the change into industrial capitalism came what is now called either *monopoly capitalism* or *imperialistic capitalism*.

The distinctions between various historical forms of capitalism are not always clear. That is because the Industrial Revolution and the development of capitalism were processes not events. They took place over centuries. Some historians even refer to an Industrial Revolution of the thirteenth century. The dividing lines between feudalism and capitalism as well as between the various stages of capitalism are somewhat imprecise. Capitalism is not easily defined even historically.

"The form which capitalism has taken in the 20th century is very different from what it was in the 19th century, so different, in fact, that it is doubtful whether even the same term should be applied to both systems." Capitalism "changes constantly to a point where the word scarcely has definable meaning." These observations highlight the problem of definition. It is not necessary to analyze capitalism's transformation or to predict what might follow, but it is necessary to be aware of the changes. Defining capitalism is an attempt to make the dynamic static. The profit motive is obviously a necessary consideration, but it is far from the only one. It existed long before the arrival of capitalism. The craftsman of the early craft guilds "sold his products retail in the town market. (It wasn't until) the acts of production and of retail sale came to be separated in space and time by the intervention of a wholesale merchant who advanced money for the purpose of wares with the object of subsequent sale at a profit [that] capitalism could be regarded as being present." Obtaining profit has resulted from different approaches at different times.

Capitalism is "'a system of exchange economy' in which the 'orienting principle of economic activity is unrestricted profit' (with the) additional characteristic that such a system is marked by a differentiation of the population into 'owners and property less workers.'" "Capital needs a class of poor people, more specifically people who do not own any means of production."

It is not only the authors of pedestrian textbooks who have difficulties with defining capitalism. Even those who attempt to do the requisite analysis face them. There is a difference, however. The apologists of capitalism usually are not among those who have attempted to do that requisite analysis.

Entrepreneurship, the factor of production that risks its resources to organize the other factors, is not by itself a sufficient condition to define capitalism either. Though widely scattered, there were sophisticated factories created and managed by entrepreneurs who brought the factors of production together long before capitalism became the major mode of production. They often included extensive and expensive capital equipment. Naturally, these entrepreneurs expected a return on their capital. After all, they put it at risk just as do present-day entrepreneurs. Admittedly these undoubtedly capitalist activities were not widespread, but they were well established.

The existence of a market is not sufficient either. Market here means an actual physical market not the abstract concept of the economist. In any case, markets also existed long before the coming of capitalism. In fact, it was the continued existence of markets that kept economic activity alive through the so called Dark Ages. Further, the existence of market socialism, as inadequate an economic system as some capitalists claim it to be, shows that it is possible for a market to exist without capitalism.

Capitalism blossomed with the Enlightenment, a period during which all social ideas "were centered around one hope: that man, in the course of his history, can liberate himself from poverty, ignorance, and injustice, and that he can build a society of harmony, peace, of union between man and man, and between man and nature." It was a period in which the primacy of the individual was advocated as an absolute. It was believed that every man being a knave must be governed by his private interest, "and, by means of it, make him, not withstanding his insatiable avarice and ambition, cooperate to public good."

The advocacy of the individual as an absolute is understandable considering the struggles with the state for personal liberty that had been occurring for centuries all over Europe. There had been "major revolutions in virtually all western states." The idea of personal liberty would soon become sacrosanct just as had the idea of the divine right of kings before it. Individual rights, along with capitalism, would develop into an extremely rigid ideology.

The struggle for individual political power almost always was associated with the development of the bourgeoisie. It just wasn't possible to carry on capitalistic activity without political and economic freedom. As the bourgeoisie grew in numbers and strength, political power began to shift away from the previously all-powerful state to the bourgeoisie, the result being that the state adjusted. The previously all powerful state compromised with the new economic class. The state mostly allowed the members of this new economic class complete power in the economic realm and provided the political liberties needed in order to function as capitalists. Even so, the assumption that the individual is absolute needs a defense..

Both society and the economy were developing rapidly during the Enlightenment, and this development needed to be justified.

It was to Adam Smith that this task fell, and he made the *invisible hand* the justification. "Every individual necessarily labors to render the annual revenue of the society as great as he can. He generally, indeed, neither intends to promote the public interest, nor knows how much he is promoting it. By preferring the support of domestic to that of foreign industry, he intends only his own security; and by directing that industry in such a manner as its produce may be of the greatest value, he intends only his own gain, and he is in this, as in many other cases, led by an invisible hand to promote an end which was no part of his intention." It has been forgotten, however, that Smith's invisible hand was not a justification of the right of the individual to do as one pleased. Neither was it an apologist's defense of unbridled capitalism. Smith believed that capitalism was necessary if a people were to have a wealthy nation. By the wealth of a nation, he meant the Gross National Product per capita. He believed that it was necessary to have a materially wealthy nation so that the nation could defend itself and so that its citizens could prosper. The purpose of a healthy and wealthy nation was to enhance the life of the individual. This is why Smith was seeking the causes of national wealth and why his great work was entitled An Inquiry into the Nature and Causes of THE WEALTH OF NATIONS as opposed to An Inquiry into the Nature and Causes of THE WEALTH OF INDIVIDUALS. Further, the *invisible hand* was not an economic concept but a theological one. It was introduced and explained not in THE WEALTH OF NATIONS but in The Theory of Moral Sentiments. In Moral Sentiments, Smith saw individuals as partners of God who would aid God in bringing society into a state of natural harmony.

He also believed that the market would affect the individual's self-interests such that each would act in a socially responsible way. Thus, private interests would be channeled into socially responsible behavior giving us a self-regulating, hence cost-free, mechanism for allocating economic resources as society wished them allocated.

Under this *laissez faire* market system, both individual liberty and the wealth of the nation would then flourish. This is why Smith believed that the type of society that he judged best was obtainable only through capitalism which allowed individuals to seek their own self-interests.

However, Smith did not adequately defend his claims. He did little more than assume the *invisible hand* based upon the assumptions that economic relations were natural and harmonious. Neither did he ever defend his naturalism.

Capitalism needs a better defense than either Smith or anyone else has ever given it. Capitalism probably is not the economic system that bests provides the best society even though its defenders still assert that it is. The market economy gives results that contradict both the reasons Smith gave for advocating the system in the first place and the reasons that current defenders present. The reality of the matter is quite different from the claims made by capitalism's proponents.

Capitalism claims to be the first economic system that even began to allow for even simple survival for the many. At that time, nature was still bountiful, and our numbers were few enough that they were not yet pushing it beyond "the tolerance margins which benign nature always provides." The population of Europe was at low ebb. "Almost everywhere in Europe, populations had increased little during most of the 17th century." "No century since the 14th has a worse record for epidemic disease." They were relatively so few people in the eighteenth and nineteenth centuries that nature was still able to take care of everybody without too much strain. The United States and other sparsely populated countries were more than able to absorb emigrants from Europe's eventual burgeoning population thus delaying the apparently inevitable Malthusian moment of truth that we now face.

The claim that capitalism was able to ensure simple survival for the many is debatable, but even if true, it is not the same as saying that under the same favorable conditions another system could not have done equally well or better or that a new system could not do even better now. Rapid economic growth was experienced, but growth rates could possibly have been even more rapid if a system other than capitalism had been employed. Alternatively, the growth rate could have been slower and more deliberate, it could have considered costs of growth that capitalism ignored and avoided many of the problems that currently confront us.

An alternate approach could have produced a superior result. Anything could have happened.

Even if such rapid growth was desirable, it must be remembered that high growth rates usually are possible only when the base is small. It is much more difficult to double a large quantity than a small one. The rapid growth rate achieved by capitalism no longer can be accomplished by any economic system. Any possible chance for an economic system other than capitalism to prove that it could have done equally well or better has been lost. It is unlikely that the base will ever be small enough again, particularly relative to the resources that were available then, for any other economic system to match capitalism's past accomplishments.

That, however, is not the point. The point is that to claim the achievements of capitalism as proof for the efficacy of the system requires more defense than is usually given.

Capitalist apologists claim that capitalism through the profit motive has raised the standards of material living of the many far better than any other system could have done. These apologists continue to claim that capitalism is still able to ensure simple survival for everyone in spite of all evidence that it cannot.

It wasn't too long ago that almost everybody still believed that "the vast majority, and soon all men, in the western world will be primarily concerned with living, [rather] than with the struggle to secure the material conditions for living." Even to Karl Marx, capitalism was "the source of expanding wealth and the backbone of technological progress [which] rescued a considerable part of the population from the idiocy of rural life."

These hopes have not materialized. "The U. S. Bishops Ad Hoc Committee on Catholic Social Teaching and the U.S. Economy" has recently said, "The fact that more than 15 percent of our nation's population lives below the official poverty level is a social and moral scandal that must not be ignored. The distribution of income and wealth in the United States is so inequitable that it violates the minimum standard of distributive justice." "On the one hand, people have attained an unheard of abundance which is given to waste, while on the other hand so many live in such poverty, deprived of the basic necessities, that one is hardly able even to count the victims of malnutrition." The persistence of an economic system that has generated such results should cause people to express moral outrage.

Further, there is the question of how our material abundance has really affected our standard of living. Economists advise us not to confuse the Gross National Product with an improved standard of living. There is more to a high standard of living than large amounts of material goods. Despite the warnings, mainstream economists still advocate growth even at greater and greater ecological costs.

The claim that capitalism still can provide for even simple survival, though more is usually claimed, is rapidly becoming less defensible. The world population continues its crazy and unrestrained growth spiral accompanied by increasing worldwide famine despite the fact that United States farmers are going bankrupt because they are producing too much food and cannot survive even with the subsidies they receive for keeping their land idle. This coexistence of starvation and plenty is not solely a distribution problem as is so often claimed. It is inherent in the system.

Even considering the advances that have been made in economic theory and all the changes that have taken place in the world in the last century, Marx's interpretation of capitalism is still the best one. "Marx's first defining feature of capitalism was that the market coordinated and allocated social labor by mediating all productive relationships among workers in such a way that the social nature of labor appeared as the price of commodities." "There were no factors of production before capitalism. Labor, land, and capital were not commodities for sale." "The creation of factors of production meant the end of assured livelihoods." The peasant *owned* his own labor power. Wealth was now in the form of capital to be used for further profit. Its previously primary use for luxury was greatly diminished.

2 EFFICIENCY

An argument given for embracing capitalism is that it is the economic system that will best achieve the greatest possible amount of social welfare. It is also claimed that capitalism is the most efficient economic system. Efficiency is a concern because it is a necessary condition if the greatest amount of social welfare is to be obtained.

"As a concept, efficiency has an intuitive appeal, but on close examination it turns out to be somewhat elusive." It appears reasonable to claim that an economic system that produces what its members want and does so without waste while creating a better society at the same time is an efficient system and should be adopted. Capitalist defenders imply that capitalism is efficient and also creates a better society, but analysis confusion and omission. They say that their economic system is efficient in every sense, but it is not. The system is not even as efficient in those areas which supposedly are its greatest strengths.

Their assumption needs to be defended.

First, *efficiency* must be defined. Various texts define one type of efficiency, technical efficiency, in different ways. Other texts fail to distinguish at all between technical efficiency and another type, economic efficiency. One text says that technical efficiency is "the utilization of the cheapest production technique for any given output rate; no inputs are willfully wasted." Another says that "it is production on the production possibilities frontier curve," the "curve that depicts all possible combinations of total output for an economy" such that all available resources are being used when production takes place on the production possibilities frontier curve. This is a major disagreement. In one case, production is technically efficient. In the other, it can be technically inefficient.

Under capitalism, production seldom takes place on the production possibilities frontier curve, and then only for a short time. Even in perfect competition, it is not insured. It is, at best, only a long-run possibility. Production will be purposely curtailed inside the limits of the curve when it is more profitable to do so. To produce on the production possibilities frontier curve, to be technically efficient, in other market structures is irrational.

Producing on the production possibilities frontier curve must obviously be the goal because it is just plain silly to defend a level of production as being efficient when there are idle resources available, particularly if it is labor that is unemployed as laborers may be having difficulties surviving. Even this definition, however, is insufficient to convey a complete sense of efficiency. It is possible that what is being produced with technical efficiency is useless or unwanted. This makes the notion of economic efficiency necessary.

Economic efficiency presents the same problem as did technical efficiency. Again, some texts define it differently from others, while still others fail to distinguish between economic and technical efficiency. One text defines economic efficiency as "the use of resources that generate the highest possible value of output as determined in the market economy by consumers." Another text says that economic efficiency "is fulfilling consumer preferences by producing the combination of goods that people want with their present income" plus technical efficiency, production on the possibilities frontier curve. "Economic efficiency is synonymous with Pareto Optimality," the condition that exists in a social organization when no change can be implemented that will make someone better off without making someone else worse off each in his or her own estimate." Pareto Optimality is another concept which itself needs to be defended. It rarely is.

This latter definition must be preferred since (1) only it assumes, by the inclusion of technical efficiency, that no resources are idle; and (2) an economic system cannot be said to be economically efficient in the manner intended if the amount of goods being produced is less than would be produced in an economy that was perfectly competitive.

So, efficiency is production both on and inside of the production possibilities frontier curve, producing a quantity desired by the consumers both under and not under perfectly competition conditions. At least one of these alternatives is impossible. Production in capitalism rarely takes place on the production possibilities frontier curve, yet producing there is the only place that is efficient.

This confusion doesn't even address social efficiency where the system is doing what the system says it should be doing thus fulfilling its stated goals. The goals of a socially efficient economic system will be determined in advance by the system which is being judged. A system should accomplish its goals if it is to be socially efficient. This is irrespective of any other type of efficiency it might have achieved.

3   COMPETITION and MONOPOLY

The capitalist model, like every model, is based upon assumptions. The capitalist model, however, is flawed. Many of its assumptions are false or contradict other assumptions. Most economists have left these assumptions unchallenged. E. F. Schumacher was an exception. His "deliberate intention was to subvert 'economic science' by calling its every assumption into question, right down to its psychological and metaphysical foundations." Most economists have had their training in the Samuelson tradition, which "merely offers up unexplained, unsubstantiated assertions." Since few question these assertions, these are in need of challenge.

The terms *capitalism* and *perfect competition* are often interchanged. No one believes that capitalism and perfect competition are synonymous, yet the terms are   used that way. This interchanging, treating them as if they were synonymous, causes results peculiar to perfect competition to appear to be the results of capitalism in general. Thus, capitalism is praised because results peculiar to perfect competition are praised. But, modern capitalism is not competitive, quite the contrary. This interchanging of *names* is confusing and incorrect.

Perfect competition is not identical to capitalism The terms are interchanged because the model of perfect competition can be defended to some degree while modern capitalism can be defended only as patchwork orthodoxy. To resolve this confusion, it will be necessary to analyze the models of market structures.

A problem with the market structure perfect competition is that its assumptions are unrealistic. It is just as confusing as the definition of capitalism. Further, one *standard* model often differs substantially from other *standard* models.

The least confusing is given by Randall Bartlett in <u>Economic Foundations of Political Power</u>. It is the one we will mostly follow, but with slight variations.

Perfect competition does not mean that the system is *perfect*. It merely means that all mutually beneficial transactions are completed. *Competition* means that each firm will minimize its costs while maximizing production as well as, or better than, its competitors, if it expects to earn a profit and remain in business. Non-price competition, advertising, is not allowed. It is a characteristic of monopolistic competition.

Standard economic theory asserts that each economic actor operates in his own self-interest, is rational, and possesses complete, or at least adequate, information, or as some say, all are possessed of equal ignorance. Other assumptions are that all products are entirely homogeneous, that entry into and exit out of the market is easy, and that there are enough producers and consumers so that no one of them, or grouping of them, can influence price. This last is supposed to ensure consumer sovereignty, the idea that "the basic decisions about what to produce and how much to produce are dominated by consumers." There also must be private property, the factor of production capital, the tools we use to produce.

Private property does not include personal belongings, individual property for use. It does not mean consumer goods. They are by definition non-productive, and therefore excluded. Using *private property* this way is peculiar to economics. It may be confusing to those who are used to the colloquial meaning. Nonetheless, that is the way economists use the term.

Private property is essential to capitalism. It is the system's most distinguishing characteristic. The system cannot exist without it. Capitalists see the right to private property as inviolable. But, it is not. Property is everywhere a creation of society. Property cannot exist without the state. The state both defines and legitimizes. Property is a social concept as well as an individual one.

Another assumption of the model is that government should be *laissez faire*, non-interference of the political entity in the economic sphere. This assumption is more of the political than it is one of capitalism. Nonetheless, it is assumed that it is necessary that the economic system be allowed to operate in an unfettered way.

Following is a list of the model's assumptions: (1) private property; (2) many buyers and many sellers; 3) free markets; (4) mobility of capital;(5) homogeneous products; (6) no non-price or cutthroat competition; (7) consumer sovereignty; (8) self-interest; (9) rationality; (10) complete, or at least adequate, information; (11) a laissez-faire government. These assumptions cannot be accepted at face value. They need to be analyzed and critiqued.

The assumption that all products in an industry are homogeneous is necessary if each individual producer is to face a perfectly elastic demand curve without which there cannot be consumer sovereignty. However, most products are heterogeneous rather than homogenous.

Homogeneous products do exist in a few industries, but never in uninformed markets, markets in which the consumer has relatively little information about the product. Even in those few industries, producers do their best to change their products so that they will gain an advantage over other producers. This is called product differentiation, the essential feature of monopolistic competition, not of perfect competition.

When producers differentiate their product by improving it, society may benefit. However, producers often seek only superficial or meaningless product differentiation. They will do almost anything to convince consumers that their product is different. They *improve* products because such changes enhance their market share and control over the amount produced. Control over supply enables them to increase profits.

This is neither economically efficient nor socially efficient. It is, at best, technically efficient, and technical efficiency by itself is inadequate to support an overall claim of efficiency.

 Recently, some consumer goods began to be produced with a high degree of isolation, their consumption has "a minimal direct and observable impact on the average consumer." Though this is seen mostly in the production of public goods like military systems, it is also seen in the private sector. Isolation in the production of private goods exists particularly when new products like sugar enhanced foods are introduced for which there wasn't a prior *need*, the *need* being created through advertising only after it was determined that production of this *new* product would be profitable. These new products obviously are not responses to consumer demand.

Most economists support mainstream consumer behavior theory. When confronted with modern advertising, which conflicts with the theory, either they will attempt to ignore the conflict or to adroitly side-step it, adroitly at least from the perspective of the not-quite-so-observant. They have not considered "those examples [that] show how much more realistic and convincing psychological theory is [in explaining consumer's behavior and motivation] than the economists' sweeping assumption[s]."

Scitovsky says that in addition to economic reasons for consumer behavior, there are mental and emotional ones. The producer is often aware of these mental and emotional reasons. Consumers and economists usually are not. The producer wants to know the motivation behind consumer behavior. Even a small amount of knowledge can greatly increase profits. The consumer suffers from a problem of marginal cost. A large investment in obtaining the requisite knowledge is necessary even to obtain a minimal savings. It is too costly for the consumer to be on an equal footing with the producer: Hence, uninformed markets.

The mainstream economist does not to want to know this because it would disrupt the model and reveal that consumer behavior theory is inconsistent with other assumptions.

The assumption of both the existence of homogeneous products and the absence of non-price competition is only a pedagogical device to help understand the model, but with the proviso that they have only been "selected on grounds of [their] convenience in [the] respect of simplicity in describing the model ... [and are] relevant in judging or applying the model" of perfect competition. These derivations are not to be used to support other market structures. In the others, firms do engage in non-price competition.

Assuming that all economic actors possess complete, or even adequate, information before they act is also unrealistic. Most authors of pedestrian texts discard the assumption for this reason, but they discard it, and never openly, only after they have applied it to consumer choice theory. Mainstream consumer choice theory cannot hold without this assumption. Some claim that because of the high marginal costs that consumers must pay if they are to be adequately informed relative to the benefits of being informed, it is rational to remain ignorant. The assumption can be accepted only if it is well-marked as a dangerous pedagogical device. To accept it in any other way is to create but an apparition of an assumption. It is not rational to claim that the chronically ill-informed are rational. Economists know little about consumer behavior.

The have been industries that have had many buyers and many sellers, but not lately. Agriculture was such an industry because "left alone, agricultural markets really do [did] work in something close to this deal fashion."

But, agricultural markets no longer are *left alone*. Political interference in agricultural markets, even if currently inadequate, seems to be necessary in the current capitalistic economy. Without such interference, the consumer would face an even more steeply downward sloping demand curve for his daily bread and brew than is now the case.

Further, agribusiness has grown too large. Large agricultural firms now have a stranglehold on supply, so even if left alone by the government, markets would probably no longer "work in something close to this ideal fashion." There simply are not any industries whose market structure fits this model.

Mobile capital is another unrealistic assumption. Remember, *capital* means economic capital, and it is economic capital that distinguishes the short run from the long run, the long run being that period of time in which economic capital can be changed.

By its very nature, economic capital is not mobile. It is usually specialized and not convertible for use in industries other than the one for which it was designed.

One's personal experience with capitalism has made an analysis of the assumption of self-interest more difficult. It seems to be a reasonable assumption that accurately represents the real world. But, does it? Perhaps, self-interest is a result of the capitalist market economy, not the cause of it. The market economist claims self-interest to be innate, but it might be just the result of a particular historical period.

Self-interest is not selfishness. It is "a concern with one's interest". We all have it. It is necessary for our survival. It is rational to have it. This does not mean it is necessary at all costs, particularly at the cost of one's moral values. One's moral values also *better his condition*. Selfishness, on the other hand, is exclusive concern only with one's own interest.

There are also times when the interest of the other is also in my interest, for example the others' interest in a peaceful and orderly way of life. The model doesn't consider this.

Neither can the assumption that there is, or could be, a *laissez-faire* government be accepted. It is an impossible assumption. Government, whether public or private, is ubiquitous. All government action, or inaction, "is the affirmative exercise of power from one view and the proscriptive check upon power from another." Government always supports one thing or another even if only by its inaction.

Laissez-faire has always been misrepresented as a policy. It is not, and never was, a do-nothing policy. It always was, of necessity, a policy of interference, whether active or passive. As long as there is a government, it must do either something or nothing. When it does something, it will change the status quo which will probably aid some while hindering others. When it does nothing, the status quo will be maintained which will aid some while hindering others. Either way, most governmental actions or inactions, intended or not, will promote the status of some at the expense of the status of others. This result is the very nature of the beast.

"The system of legal controls, whether employed actively through imposing state obligations or more passively through affording protection for private economic pressures, determines the nature of the economic system." It gives structure to private property as private coercive power or, more strikingly, public government creates private government.

Even more important is that. "Any particular state is the child of the class or classes of society which benefit from the particular set of property relations which it is the state's obligation to enforce." All governments rule in the interest of those who created the government. Adam Smith said the same. "Civil government, so far as it is instituted for the security of property, is in reality instituted for the defence of the rich against the poor, or of those who have some property against those who have none at all." Smith was not alone among our *heroes* who understood this. John Locke said "government has no end other than the preservation of property."

That the protection of private property is the primary concern of a government in a capitalist country is common-sensical and straight-forward. It is not likely that a group of people with enough power to form a government would form one that did not protect and promote their own interests rather than the interests of others.

The United States Constitutional Convention was all about the protection of private property. The Convention wasn't called to write a constitution, but to correct the Articles of Confederation, to correct what many saw to be an extensively democratic society. The Federalist *aristocrats* thought the people to be excessive in the exercise of their newly-granted democratic freedoms. Looking at the Convention would reveal that ultimate power was retained for the writers of the document. Only that amount of power which was absolutely necessary to maintain an acceptable level of social order was provided to anyone else. In fact, were the Articles of Confederation to be the basis of judgment, the Convention was extraconstitutionally called.

The contrast between the Declaration of Independence and the Constitution is great indeed. The former trusted the people. The latter didn't. The Electoral College, the appointment of Senators, unequal and staggered terms of office display this mistrust. White male property owners wrote the Constitution. It should not be surprising that largely only the white male property owner was granted the franchise.

The impossibility of government being *laissez-faire* should be obvious. Apparently, it is not. Friedman is an advocate of, if not *laissez-faire* government, minimal government. Yet, he maintains that the major function of government is enforcement of private contracts and fostering competitive markets.

"It is an obvious responsibility of the state … to maintain the legal and institutional framework within which competition can function effectively as an agency of control." "Government is essential both as a forum for determining the 'rules of the game' and as an umpire to interpret and enforce the rules decided on."

Acting as an umpire has been vastly exaggerated as a reason for government existing in the first place.

This is far from being *laissez faire*. Not only is it the role of government under this peculiar interpretation to do whatever is required to promote the market system, it also is its role to preserve property rights, to serve as the impartial arbiter of justice, economic and otherwise. Apparently, this is the role of all governments, since Dr. Friedman does not limit his claim to a capitalist government. Even if it was possible for *laissez-faire* to obtain, it never has.

History is full of examples showing that *laissez faire* has never been more than an ideal. It was the Crown's involvement in the wool export trade as early as the fourteenth century, an involvement due to the large export taxes received by the Crown, that led England into the Industrial Revolution. "Historically, it [*laissez faire*] developed as a vigorous attack upon entrenched social, commercial, and industrial privilege."

What the proponents of capitalism really want when they advocate for a *laissez-faire* government is not just a government that is not antagonistic towards capitalism but one which advocates towards capitalism.

In order for the model of perfect competition to show that capitalism is the best economic system, that model needs conditions that supposedly would obtain under a *laissez-faire* government. The model builders claim that this type of political and economic arrangement provides for the greatest individual freedom. They assume that the best economic system is the best economic system.

It is difficult to claim that one is acting rationally if that person doesn't have all the information needed to make a rational decision. Yet, this is what mainstream economists claim for consumer and producer alike. Because of uncertainty in the world, it is said to be rational to act without adequate information. For example, one might not have enough time to obtain adequate information when an immediate decision is necessary. It is seldom rational just to procrastinate. One must decide and hope for the best. But even if it is necessary in the short run, as it often is, in the long run, it is neither rational nor cost-effective to allow it to continue.

However, one should not often be that unprepared. If one is continuously unprepared, one cannot pretend to be rational. Even if one makes adequate short-run decisions, those short-run decisions are rational only if they fulfill long-run criteria. Short-run rationality is little more than an expediency.

Further, it is often likely that the additional information necessitated by being unprepared is such that it can be useful in a myriad of situations, thus dramatically lowering the marginal cost of obtaining it.

Limiting rationality by asserting that it is rational to act out of ignorance is to identify it with ignorance. This limitation so emasculates rationality that it becomes a thing undesirable to have. If information has any value at all, it is to serve us. To act without it is hardly rational.

Even with the *ad hoc* assumptions added to protect the integrity of the model's original assumptions, the capitalist still ends up with a system that undercuts its own assumptions, has conclusions that contradict its assumptions when it does not ignore them completely, and has results that contradict the reasons given for advocating the system. Their assumptions cannot maintain their rational integrity.

Whatever economic system a society adopts, that society must be careful that it really does get what it has selected. A society that isn't careful shouldn't be surprised with what it gets. That is what is happening now. Most citizens of the current capitalist industrialized West are enamored with this economic model, but there is no corresponding reality. Even the system's economists are not surprised that reality is not as the model predicts it should be. A senior official under President Carter said, "It's really scary. This inflation thing is frightening because we do not know what causes it, or what to do about it. The economists go to their computers, plug in the data, and out comes information that says nothing like this should be happening. It's very, very scary stuff."

Yes, it's scary. But, it's even scarier that economists are surprised that reality does not map on the predictions of their model. They should be surprised if it did. Reality is too complicated to be accurately predicted by a model. The scariest thing of all is that those surprised economists maintain their belief in their model in spite of all evidence to the contrary.

OTHER MARKET STRUCTURES

A monopoly is when one firm is the entire industry. An oligopoly is when there are relatively few firms in a given industry which produce a relatively large percentage of the industry's total production. A monopolistic competitive market is when there are a significant number of sellers producing similar but differentiated products and who aggressively advertise those differences. Perfect competition doesn't exist today, if it ever did. The other market structures, on the other hand, reflect capitalism's reality. It is necessary, therefore, to understand them and to compare them to the capitalists' claims.

These other market structures are different, but the same. A common element in all of them is that the individual firm faces a downward sloping demand curve. Though the slope of that curve and of its accompanying marginal cost curve may vary, the principle is the same. Facing a downward sloping demand curve allows a firm to affect the price of its product in an upward direction by limiting supply, the amount of the supply limitation and the price control being determined by the amount of market control the firm has.

Such firms are price-makers, they are able to set the market price, at least partially, because of their market control as opposed to price-takers, firms that are forced to take the market price as given because it is exogenously determined. Under perfect competition, all firms are price-takers. All others are price-makers because they have some degree of monopoly control by virtue of a downward sloping demand curve. This is but an explanation of mainstream microeconomics.

"Marshall took the world as it is; he sought to construct an 'engine' to analyze it, not a photographic reproduction of it. In analyzing the world as it is, Marshall constructed the hypothesis that, for many problems, firms could be grouped into 'industries' such that the similarities among the firms in each group were more important than the differences among them." Marshall's models have extremely high degrees of explanatory power. Further, they are very realistic.

All capitalist firms, irrespective of market structure, produce or attempt to produce at that point where marginal revenue equals marginal cost, where the last dollar of return exactly equals the last dollar spent on production. It is here that profit maximization, the goal of the firm is reached.

In deciding how much to produce, a firm will consider only those costs and benefits it actually experiences. There is in almost every industry what are called externalities, spillovers, or neighborhood effects. An externality exists where there is a cost or a benefit that is external to an exchange, where some costs and/or benefits accrue to a party or parties other than the parties immediate to the transaction. An example of an externality is pollution in the production process. Rather than pay the cost of not polluting, the firm pollutes.

Negative externalities are those where those externalities are a cost to the party ultimately forced to bear them. Positive externalities are those externalities which are a benefit to the party ultimately allowed to enjoy them. Negative externalities are the large majority of externalities under capitalism. If the production process results in a positive externality, it will surely have been unintended. If it results in a negative externality, the result is less likely to have been unintended. If one is operating in order to maximize profit, one will be more apt to pay close attention to retaining that which would be a revenue than to that which would be a cost.

Known positive externalities are always unintended because as soon as one is recognized an attempt will be made to internalize it. With negative externalities, the opposite is the case. Every effort will be made to keep them external. The superior manager also will attempt to make as many of the internal costs external as possible even if they don't naturally occur that way. If it will increase profits, the production process will be altered to externalize costs. In addition to these negative externalities, there are other social costs with which the individual producer is not concerned. If a firm is a price-maker, there is purposeful underproduction. Underproduction results in higher costs for consumers.

This underproduction results in a misallocation of resources, particularly in resources being underutilized. These externalities, underproduction and misallocation of resources are market imperfections or market failures and are the rule, not the exception. There are many transactions desired by the consumer that the market forbids. People need and want to work, but the market may forbid them from doing so because it is not profitable to increase production. The result is high unemployment rates.

Unemployment is the result when a producer limits production. Competition in the real-world market is cutthroat, non-price and noxious. Misallocation and underutilization of resources are imperfections, but they are not failures. A failure is not, or should not be, the expected result of the system.

With capitalism, these imperfections are not incidental anomalies. They are the rule. These social costs are inevitable when decisions are made by some microeconomic units, individual firms operating in their own self-interests with little or no regard for the other microeconomic units. These are individual workers. Costs are also incurred by the macro economy. The individual micro-units causing them enjoy the benefits.

Perfect competition doesn't exist. It is monopolistic competition, oligopoly, and monopoly which are real. None of them really reflects the alleged ideology of the capitalist.

4 FREE MARKET

Capitalism often is referred to as the competitive free enterprise system or the free market system The market is not nearly as socially beneficial as capitalism claims it to be.

A difficulty with the market is that it is dominated by price-maker firms. "Pure [perfect] competition is a relatively rare market structure in our economy. There are few industries which more closely approximate the competitive model than they do any other market structure."

The reason given for this model is that "pure [perfect] competition provides the simplest context in which to apply the revenue and cost concepts. ... Pure [perfect] competition is a clear and meaningful starting point for any discussion of price and output determination. ... A purely [perfectly] competitive economy provides us with a standard, or norm, against which the efficiency of the real-world economy can be compared and evaluated." "Free markets are like an objective ideal."

The free market isn't free. "Law [government] is an instrument for the attainment of economic objectives and the economy is an object of legal control. The economy [is] a system of mutual coercion predicated upon an understanding that power is the critical variable for an adequate comprehension of the organization and structure of the economic system."

Capitalism is said to have been designed to promote the individual. "Individual men are [after all] necessarily the foundation, cause, and end of all social institutions." Yet "as an economic agency, markets establish the opposite of solidarity -- they declare the war of each against all." The market doesn't bring out the best in people. It brings out the worst. "There could be ... only temporary truce." Contrary to the stated purposes of the market system, it is the few against the many. That's all there ever is.

Neither is the free market necessary. The world is one of scarcity and therefore one of choice. "Almost all, indeed perhaps all, choice is constrained choice; each person is constrained by the coercive impact of the choices made by others, singly or through collective choice." The market seems to be a natural outgrowth of that constraint and the necessarily constrained choices. It provides a process by which those constrained choices can be made. But the market system is not a natural outgrowth. It "is [only] one possible institution for coordinating economic activities of disparate groups of people." It is generally assumed that the market is non-coercive, but it is not.

Everything about the operation of the market economy is necessarily coercive. "There [is] coercion generic to even a supposedly noncoercive economic system." *Coercion*, when used in this way is a neutral term. Coercion is ubiquitous because it is necessary. It is not an evil, "though there is a permanent necessity of guarding against felt abuses."

That our choices are constrained and that the alternatives faced are givens from among which we must choose is a limitation that confronts everybody. The problem is not, as people think, one of freedom versus coercion. The problem is how to structure the necessary coercion which will dictate the structure of volitional freedom. "The [ultimate] problem is who chooses."

Neither does the market coordinate economic activity such that each item's price is an objective aggregate of the individual buyers and sellers. The market is not objective. "The word value suggests valuation by or for something, or someone." Each person decides for himself what does or does not have value for him. That valuation is based upon whatever the individual decides to base it upon. There is no universal measure that can be used to decide if the valuation is a correct one. Valuation is, and by its nature must be, subjective. The best that can be said for the market is that it objectively aggregates individual subjective valuations. Even if the market were free and competitive, it still would not be objective.

Neither does, the market give value to anything. The market only assigns an *ex post* validation of already-present value. Whatever is of value in a particular good or service exists before the market becomes involved. The market only assigns a monetary value to that already-existing value.

Neither is the market's valuation even accurate. It omits much. It suppresses "innumerable qualitative distinctions which are vital to man and society" because those distinctions, beauty, health, cleanliness, etc., are meaningless to it so the capitalistic economic calculus does not consider them.

The presence of negative externalities shows that the market doesn't consider all costs. In principle, perhaps, this flaw could be corrected with all necessary considerations brought into the economic calculus. If they were, however, the process would conflict with the power of the present mutually coercive economy. Because there are those who have been grandfathered into power, who had certain rights before those rights were legislatively or administratively removed and who will do whatever they need to do in order to maintain the existing structure of coercion, it is unlikely that meaningful change will ever occur if the current structure is maintained as it is presently constituted.

Neither is the market efficient. Efficiency means that the market quickly provides the information needed to make correct choices. It doesn't. There are many market imperfections.

The unaided market cannot achieve any *efficient* efficiency. Imperfect competition exists everywhere as do significant negative externalities and increasing returns to scale.

Further, how is the market supposed to supply public goods "goods and services having the properties that (1) they cannot be provided to one citizen without being provided also to that citizen's neighbors, and (2) once provided to one citizen, they can be provided to others at zero cost?" This market imperfection further undermines any claim for efficiency.

"People are social; what happens for each, affects all." The human is a social creature and can develop only in society. "All human activities are social, rather than private in their effects." The system's defenders believe that "a market system obliges its participants to be other-regarding." But, it does not. The goal of maximizing profit is a major reason that our society faces a plethora of negative externalities.

Selfishness, as opposed to rational self-interest, is another reason negative externalities exist. The capitalist economic calculus does not ever demand the other person's benefit be considered even when the other person's benefit is of overriding significance. The result is an abundance of significant market imperfections.

Negative externalities are not exceptions. They are the rule. There are also other negative externalities which are not considered. In a market economy, if there is a social cost to a transaction, the participants in that transaction, if they are profit-maximizers, will ignore those costs if they are not directly inflicted on them or not somehow forced to bear them.

"Markets hide from consideration the actual concrete human costs and gains that accrue from economic activities." They overestimate a product's worth when they ignore the effect of the transactions upon the rest of us. The market acts as if there were only one consumer. The other participants in the transaction are ignored. Those who are not immediate participants don't count. Yet, others are affected by the actions of the other. In this sense, all goods are public. Since those who are not direct participants are not considered, the market cannot be expected to produce accurate prices.

So, markets not only limit their concern to the directly involved participants, they also set those participants off against one another. "Neither participant is concerned with the human situation of the other." Markets prohibit cooperation as irrational. They "systematically establish false contradictions between individual and societal well-being." Markets embody "individualism of the worse type, [noxious] competition and greed." "In providing for your pleasure, I fleece you."

The standard argument used to defend capitalism is the same as was used by Adam Smith. Capitalism allows individuals to operate in one's own self-interest, and when individuals do so in a perfectly competitive market structure, the best society results. That world does not exist and never did. The defense was inadequate then. It still is. Using the conclusions of the standard model to advocate capitalism is stretching self-interest beyond credulity. To make such a claim is absurd.

"Competition was always … very imperfect … a dangerous myth." Economic actors operate in their own self-interest in an attempt to increase their security frequently delimiting competition. "In the real world, virtually all markets are 'imperfect' in various ways."

Real-world capitalism is not competitive. Perfect competition is not real. Monopoly, oligopoly, monopolistic competition are real. They are not competitive. Why would anyone ever think that capitalism was competitive?

"It is a mistake to believe that businessmen actually want a completely free market. It is a natural temptation for them to protect whatever advantages they have" and to extend them, politically if necessary. Ideally, they seek monopoly for themselves in the sale of their products and seek "a completely free market," if not a monopsony, being the only buyer of a particular factor of production. A monopsonistic firm will generate a profit from buying an input from a competitive supplier just as it will generate a profit from labor power if the workers are not truly free to bargain. The monopsonistic firm will buy factors of production in a competitive market and then selling what is produced in a monopolistic market giving it the largest possible positive difference between the cost of production and the price charged for what is produced, and hence the largest possible profit.

There is an "inevitable tendency for everyone to be in favor of a free market for everyone else, while regarding himself as deserving of special treatment." "Businessmen who complain about governmental regulations which they don't like are the first to ask for regulations which they do like--because the latter protect their own interests and penalize competitors." "The Capitalist has two tongues in his mouth; he uses the one at buying, the other at selling." Capitalists fear competition because "the possibility of success will naturally be accompanied by the possibility of failure." "The market, [even when it is not perfectly competitive] involves a continual possibility of competitive failure and thus creates basic insecurities."

Particularly today with the great size of the modern corporation, "the very size of capital investment [read *risk*] makes it necessary not to leave consumption to chance." "As long as the economic security is not guaranteed, it [the individual firm] is likely to function to protect [and out of security, to extend] its own special status-quo interests--even when they run counter to the broader interests of society." Yet, mainstream economists still talk as if the opposite were the case.

The market system is not what it is claimed to be. It creates significant social harm. Significant changes are necessary.

Because labor must be free to contract if the market is to adequately allocate resources, it is claimed that the market gives labor the freedom to contract. But, labor seldom is free to *fairly* contract. Property is almost always superior in strength to labor. This strength allows that more powerful sector to coerce the others. It is difficult to view this as contributing to a superior society.

Economics texts have chapters "The Supply and Demand for Productive Resources" or "Factor Markets and Marginal Productivity Theory." The labor supply of the individual is thought of in the same terms consumer choice is thought of. It is "a trade-off between two sources of utility\--leisure and the consumption of purchased goods and services. The hourly wage rate can be thought of as the price--or more precisely as the opportunity cost--of leisure to the worker."

Voluntary, or complete, freedom exists only when one can make choices unconstrained by others. Voluntary freedom is choosing between alternatives that you present to yourself. Volitional freedom is choosing between alternatives limited by the presence or actions of others. It is a lesser freedom. Where there is more than one person, there is necessarily only volitional freedom. Each person is a constraint upon the other. "This [impact] of the behavior and/or choices of others is coercion which may take many forms and is generally a matter of degree, but always affects the range and/or degree of possible realization and/or cost of alternatives."

Social institutions are arranged or constructed in a certain way, but they need not be as they are. They are not neutral. They are what they are for some reason, and they are often unobtrusive. Their existence is taken for granted. "Indeed, legal coercion itself is generally unrecognized in the status quo because it is unobtrusive and taken for granted ... Whatever is perceived as improper is called coercion. That which is not seen as improper is simply accepted."

Private property is such an accepted institution, unobtrusive and taken for granted. It is simply accepted as it is found. Attacks on it are seen as improper. But, private property is not neutral. It is coercive. If you possess private property, you not only have greater volitional freedom concerning actions that only affect yourself, you also have greater volitional freedom in that you can use that private property to coerce others.

Whatever else government might be, whether private or public, it is a proscriptive check upon voluntary freedom. It constrains choice. Government is a "system of power and pressure which has coercive impact on the resultant pattern of volitional freedom." The institution of private property fits this definition.

Those who control property have power over others. Having that power enables them to govern others just as public officials do. Government, then, includes both the public and the private sectors. Again, so much for the normally constructed assumption of *laissez faire*.

A new definition of price emerges from this analysis. Price is that which must be paid to release one's withholding capacity. This is what occurs when   property and labor *bargain*. Property withholds its productive capacity from labor until labor agrees to sell itself for as little as property can bring labor to accept. "Withholding of what another wants as the penalty for non-compliance is the essence of bargaining power."

Granted, the scenario can be reversed. Labor can withhold its productive capacity from property until property agrees to pay labor as much as labor can bring it to pay. A major difference, however, is that the owners of property may leave it idle and still survive. They needn't use it in production or even liquidate some of it. They can survive.

Labor, on the other hand, cannot survive without using its productive capacity. Property has the overwhelming advantage in this process of mutual coercion called bargaining.

Labor's so-called freedom to contract is little more than volitional freedom imposed upon it by power, which is "establishing one's own alternatives and defending against the exposure which one has to others' freedom." To be sure, the process is in some sense bargaining, but it is bargaining between nonequals. Property is stronger in this process than is labor. Labor is not free to contract in any real sense of the word *free*.

Mainstream consumer choice theory is not true. Neither is labor being free to contract. Little of what is called *freedom* is voluntary freedom, "complete autonomy with the absence of constrained choice or limits to choice or behavior." What we normally call freedom is volitional freedom, "circumstantially limited exercise of choice between alternatives or behavior."

5   PROFIT and *LAISSEZ FAIRE*

Capitalism claims that individuals seeking profit create social benefits that would not otherwise exist. This *invisible hand* argument and profit both require analysis.

Profit is thought of as the difference between revenue and expenses. This concept of profit is correct only if all costs, both explicit and implicit, are included.. Implicit expenses are "opportunity costs to a firm of using resources owned by the firm itself or contributed by owners of the firm." The major implicit cost is the opportunity cost of capital, the amount of interest that the money invested in a business could have earned had it been invested elsewhere. That cost is not explicitly included in the company's costs. It should be.

The labor contributed by an owner without direct reimbursement is also an implicit cost. All costs must be considered. Otherwise, the economic profit can't be computed.

A balance sheet profit is not *true* profit. The omitted cost of implicit expenses must be subtracted. Economic profit is the remainder of revenue after subtracting all expenses, explicit and implicit. The result is the *true* profit, the economic profit. If the result is zero, economists call it a *normal* profit.

"Are economic profits ever justified?" Capitalists say the self-interested profit motive creates the best society. Critics say profits are the result of the exploitation of labor. "Exploitation exists because the extra value contributed by labor is exploited by the capitalist." "The cause of profit is that labor produces more than is required for its support."

Just as the defenders are required to justify their claims, so are the critics. Profit can result from other sources such as invention, innovation or simply risk taking. These alternatives are seldom considered by the critic.

Further, some claim that production and any profit that results from it are a function of society. Thus, society has some claim to that profit and the right to redistribute it.

Irrespective of the economic system, it is a principle of economics that the use of any resource has an opportunity cost, the value of the next most desired but sacrificed alternative. This includes capital irrespective of the mode of that capital's ownership. In every case, there is an opportunity cost of capital irrespective of whether the capital is owned privately, as under capitalism, or collectively, as in the Soviet economy. Irrespective of the economic system, resources will not be expended unless the return from its use is at least equal to that which could be received from its best alternative use. Otherwise, it would be used in the alternate situation where the return would be larger. This does not consider any non-economic reasons for otherwise expending capital. Capital, in all economic systems, should always expect a profit, a normal one perhaps, but a profit nonetheless.

In capitalism, economic profit remains in the hands of the capitalist. Should it? Which factor of production should receive it, capital or labor? Or, the State? Distribution is determined by the ability to coerce.

Having explained *normal profit*, it is necessary to ask whether *economic profit* is justified. Economic profit can result in several different ways other than the usual.

First, economic profit can result from invention, innovation, discovery of a new material or process, or simply risk taking. Whatever that *something* new might be, it is almost always a result of human capital, education or skill, which are forms of labor. The resulting economic profit is then justified as a return to labor. Justifying economic profit is not as easy, if it is the result of an accidental rather than a purposeful act.

Second, economic profit might result from entrepreneurial activities. Someone may observe a social need no one else had seen and move to fill it. Again, the new product or service is a result of human capital and might be justified in the same way as was the preceding.

Then, there is the economic profit earned by a Boulton, profit that results from funds invested in somebody else's invention, discovery, or entrepreneurship. Investment involves risk. There is more to consider than just the opportunity cost of capital. Not only is there a return for the opportunity cost of capital, there also must be a return to reward the investors for putting their money at risk.

Lastly, there is the economic profit that results from market control where that market control is not the result of the recipient's own endeavors. An example of this is the windfall profits enjoyed by the oil companies when the O.P.E.C. nations increased the price of their oil. As predicted by the principle of marginal pricing, the principle that all sales take place at the price of the last sale, the price of all oil increased. This resulted in large windfall profits for oil companies who had been holding those resources at that time. They did nothing to earn it except control resources and distribution.

"The [usual] fundamental justification for profit rests on a social decision, one that was never really made, to confer rewards on those who have resources if they abstain from consuming them in order to invest them in the creation of new industries."

This might sound reasonable, but it was not how capital sufficient for industrial investment really was accumulated. In England where capitalism first took hold to produce the Industrial Revolution, it was the activities of the English Crown that made the predominance of the wool industry possible. The Crown knew the value of the country's wool industry, and it levied high export duties on the wool without adversely affecting demand, such was the wool's high quality. The Crown did everything that it could to protect and promote the industry. This also resulted in high profits for the industry itself. None of these high profits were the result of abstaining from consumption. They were a largesse received under the protection of the Crown.

Thus, large reservoirs of capital were created, but they were not always forthcoming because the principle of limited liability was not yet very widespread.

Another justification for profits is that "the existence of profits signals quickly whether resources are being used in a creative, dynamic way or in a useful way. As a reward for enterprise, profits signal new creativity and efficiency." They do not. Look at what modern capitalism has done to our biological capital, "the irreplaceable capital which man has not made, but simply found, and without which he can do nothing." Capitalism is depleting it. This is neither creative or efficient, but it does produce economic profit for the capitalist.

Since biological capital is not a direct cost to the producer, the producer treats the return from its use as an income item rather than as an expense item to be used in restoring it to its previous condition. Restoring capital to its previous condition after use is what the producer does to their invested capital. Some of the producer's return is a depreciation expense else the capitalist would soon be without capital. Regarding biological capital, however, the producer uses it up in the process of making larger economic profits.

This is not an argument based on the need to protect the environment, though it well could be. It is based solely on ignored costs. The costs are there, and the current economic calculus ignores them. Further, there is a distinct difference between the short-run costs of the replaceable man-made factors of production and the long-run costs of the irreplaceable natural factors of production. The current economic calculus does not recognize the difference.

It is also claimed that "economic growth is hardly possible without profit." This claim is also debatable. But, is that growth desirable in the first place?

Lastly, most agree that "profits must be fairly earned. Their use should benefit mankind." Some say that surplus is not profit, but a *social dividend*. Much of it results from the social gift of limited liability. Thus, a social claim on the results of the activities society allows and encourages seems reasonable. However, profits are seldom *fairly earned*, so there seems to be little justification for most economic profits.

However, some profits can be justified. Thus, all profits cannot be rejected out of hand as innately objectionable.

LAISSEZ FAIRE

Milton Friedman says, "The scope of government must be limited. [But amongst] its major functions must be ... to enforce private contracts, to foster competitive markets." For an advocate of laissez *faire*, his list of government's major functions is more than just a little strange. He includes government interference in the marketplace as a proper role of government. But, he is correct. It is necessary for government to regulate the economy.

Everyone agrees that an economic system cannot do everything and that it does some things wrong. Further, most agree that it is government's place to promote the economic system over which it governs. If people don't agree that this is government's place, they at least agree that it is what government does. Further, it is sometimes agreed that government should correct those things that the economic system does wrong or can't do at all. This is what now is mostly meant by the term *laissez faire*, but it is not.

Participation in the economy has become a necessary function of government. Government is, after all, a method of consolidating and exercising power. The amount or degree of that participation is another question.

If the actions of the modern capitalists are to be restrained, only government has the power to do it. Yet, the modern capitalist has gained the power in government and uses that power in its own self-interests and to maintain its hold on that power. Government is necessary if capitalism is to function It is necessary to restrain capitalism. It is necessary to understand fully the relationship of government to capitalism.

6   ALIENATION

"In its objective sense, alienation means powerlessness or lack of control; a person is alienated from something, [a job] if he or she has no control over it." Capitalist society is so structured that almost all activities and relationships are "essentially independent of individual needs." In a society that prides itself on individualism as the capitalist economy does, denial of "life-giving and personally rewarding activities and relationships" doesn't make sense. The individual is *treated as a means rather than as an end* in himself. For all of his social attributes, desires and needs, the individual human is an individual, and an end in himself.

"Human qualities are transformed into commodities." "Capitalism puts things (capital) higher than life (labor)." The result is "the loss of the self in the aimless and unconscious creation of a world beyond the control of its creators." This is an odd result for a system that is said to so highly value individuals.

As workers are alienated from their work and their own essence as human beings by the capitalist mode of production, they lose "control over their own humanness, their potential for creative work." Thus, the worker is alienated from himself, and as the usual production process rigidly controls the on-the-job relations of a worker with his fellows and certainly separates the worker from the consumers of the workers' products, the worker is also alienated from others.

Capitalism accentuates alienation and makes it widespread. Capitalism' should recognize alienation as a cost. It does not.

7   CORPORATIONS

In the beginning, God might have created the heavens and the earth, but He did not create corporations. His creations did. And, only recently.

The current overwhelming presence of the corporation is a recent historical phenomenon. They have been with us only a one-hundred-fifty years or so. Prior to this, the corporate form was basically illegal. There were good reasons for this. The corporation is an artificial being, a creation of the state. Corporations have brought with them both great achievements and great difficulties. They have historically gone from providing society benefit to burdening it with cost.

One corporate form, the "joint-stock enterprise for trading purposes has existed in England from at least 1553." However, the joint-stock enterprise could not become a general movement "until certain economic and legal changes had been effected." The economic changes came with the beginnings of the large-scale and rapid Industrial Revolution in the latter half of the eighteenth century. The legal changes were the Registration Act of 1844, the Limited Liability Act of 1855, and the Joint Stock Companies Act of 1856. It wasn't until after these Acts of Parliament were passed that the corporate form began to proliferate.

Unincorporated joint-stock enterprise was made illegal by the Bubble Act of 1720. England had just suffered through a disastrous experience, now called the South-Sea Bubble. Because of this experience and others like them, joint-stock companies received the name of *Bubbles*. During the South-Sea Bubble, large numbers of people, many of whom were government annuitants, lost their fortunes in a mania of speculation. "Men were no longer satisfied with the slow but sure profits of cautious industry. The hopes of boundless wealth for the morrow made them heedless and extravagant for today."

This activity is not unlike much of today's speculative investment. Such social disorder is only one of the reasons why unincorporated companies were made illegal, and a special charter of incorporation was seldom granted.

Even as the South-Sea Bubble began bubbling, there were voices warning against the conditions that allowed it. It was said that "it countenanced 'the dangerous practice of stock jobbing' and would divert the genius of the nation from trade and industry. [Further,] if the plan succeeded, the directors [of the South-Sea Company] would become masters of the government, form a new and absolute aristocracy in the kingdom, and control the resolutions of the legislature." This prediction come true. Current capitalists have Citizens United.

The results of the South Sea Bubble were that "the disasters of the time probably checked of themselves any tendency of the company-form to spread generally and were a practical demonstration of its possible defects." All companies now were to operate under the English law of partnership, which was judge-made case-law unless granted a charter by Parliament. This made setting up a large joint-stock enterprise very difficult. Besides the "unlimited liability attaching to each member, [there was] the almost utter impossibility of suing and being sued. [These were always given as] the leading reasons in all petitions for corporations."

The Bubble Act was repealed in 1825. It was unintelligible. Nowhere was a clear definition of a *company* given. However, the Repealing Act did little to bring forth more firms with the modern corporate form. Nothing positive was proposed. The Repeal Act didn't do anything to liberalize the authorizing of the corporate form. All that was done was to allow the Crown, rather than Parliament, to grant the authorization. Just as before, few special charters were granted.

"With this as the state of the law, English firms must have been small partnerships. Large partnerships simply could not carry on.

Until the law was changed, full economic development was impossible." Capitalists, who were not able or otherwise inclined to enter business as active partners, had no way of safely investing any part of their wealth in productive enterprise without risking all their possessions. Firms were not going to expand very rapidly.

The argument for change was that "much capital was lying idle or not employed to the best advantage ... Poor but able men were unable to get support from richer men for these would thereby risk their entire fortunes. Not every Watt found his Boulton. Capital and enterprise were divorced and both were suffering."

It was "limited liability [that] would open the general field of industry to investments and further national prosperity. [But] limited liability was to be a right by regulations laid down by Parliament." The corporation, or the *Ltd*, is clearly a creation and gift of the state. Limited liability, like private property, is not an inviolable right.

It wasn't as if the benefits that could accrue to society under the corporate form went unrecognized. There wasn't any prohibition against limited liability under English law. It was just that it was not easy. In fact, it was made difficult. When it did occur, it was usually a matter of a negotiated contract of which all parties were knowledgeable on a first-hand basis. This virtually eliminated actions from ignorance. Further since it is difficult to negotiate contracts between a large numbers of parties, there was never a market for the shares of these ventures. This procedure eliminated the possibility of blind speculation by the masses.

A more easily obtainable corporate form was not easily won. There were many who fought against its creation. "One opponent, referring to the Bill of 1856, wrote: 'This Limited Liability Bill ought therefore to be called "An Act for the better enabling Adventurers to interfere with and ruin Established Trades without risk to themselves!"'

In the United States, the corporate form wasn't adopted widely until after the Civil War. Prior to that time, incorporation was considered a privilege granted by the state "chiefly in the formation of some project necessary for the public good, perhaps of such magnitude that the risks had to be widely distributed." The Erie Canal was one such project with a large magnitude of risk for which a corporate charter was granted by the state. Corporations were thought of largely as public institutions.

The new laws opened the general field of industry to investments which resulted in national prosperity. The same thing that happened in England also began to happen here in the United States. There was an extremely rapid growth of American industry after the Civil War. Even at the turn of the century, this growth was not showing any signs of abating. In the last decade of the nineteenth century alone, industrial production in the United States had almost doubled.

The corporate form enabled much of this growth. Unlimited liability was no longer an impediment. To become incorporated was becoming increasingly easy. Previously idle capital was now put to work. Along with technological innovations, the corporate form helped foment other changes as well. There were rapid changes in finance capital and in organizations. Each fed upon itself and upon the other resulting in even more spectacular growth. This rapid growth could not have occurred without the corporate form.

However since the rebirth of this modern-day Phoenix from the ashes of the South-Sea Bubble, there have been major problems particularly the concentration of wealth and power. Concentration in industry, in all its forms, combinations, trusts, etc., became all too apparent in the last quarter of the nineteenth century. While this great industrial concentration brought benefits, it also brought great costs. It was the corporate form that allowed this concentration of industry, of wealth, of power, and enabled even more future growth.

Corporations allowed the accumulation of capital necessary for the great economic growth being made possible by rapid scientific and technological advances. This large accumulation of capital would allow firms to take advantage of the decreasing economies of scale that technology was making possible.

Decreasing economies of scale is where costs per unit of production decrease as total production increases. Businesses began to propagandize the public to the effect that the public should be pleased that businesses have become as large as they had. This large size enabled them to take advantage of newly created economies of scale. If business could utilize these economies of scale, the public would reap rewards in the form of more, less-expensive products because there would be much lower costs of production. If such economies of scale were not allowed, the public would suffer in the form of higher prices for a lesser quantity and variety of goods.

However, firms grew larger than the size they claimed they needed to be. This greater size endowed them with the correspondingly greater economic power which enabled them better to control the amount produced and the price charged. This abuse continues. Antitrust laws and other similar efforts have been virtually toothless.

Another reason given for forming combinations was to level the ups and downs of the economy. These ups and downs were thought to be caused by the wasteful and harmful competition caused by industrial growth. Those who *favored* competition now warned us against it.

Before the Sugar Trust was formed, almost one-half of the existing firms were forced out of business because of price cutting. The reason for combining was to obtain the additional market power necessary to further maximize profits.

Even though microeconomics was then only in its infancy, the real world was not. Businessmen searched for ways to eliminate competition and to maximize profit long before economists began to explain their activities to them in terms more complicated than they could readily understand.

Analysis of these economies of scale show that they didn't always occur as propagandized. For instance, U.S. Steel's cost of production was no lower than that of its smaller competitors. When they did occur, they weren't passed on to the consumer, but were retained by the corporation in higher profits.

The argument that economies of scale justify this concentration is still being made. The evidence still does not support it. Concentration in almost every oligopolistic industry is beyond that needed for efficient operation. Some large firms may have experienced natural economies of scale, but evidence shows that few have grown this way. They were a smokescreen for the increased profits that resulted from increased control over supply. Granted, the advanced level of technology was an important enabling condition, but the advanced technology could not have been readily utilized without the corporate form. Profits were the motivation, not a desire to produce more, less-expensive products.

Besides firms having great market control for no justifiable reason, the very size of these firms causes other problems

The large size of the modern firm unit enables it to act in ways which conflict with the ecology. The environment has natural restraints that prevent certain destructive or otherwise undesirable events from occurring. Production motivated solely by the desire for large profits does not have these restraints. In fact, it creates conditions that destroy or otherwise negatively alter the ecology's natural restraints. The unnatural will die in nature if unaided in its fight for survival. Materialism, in its drive for greater profits, aids the unnatural's fight for survival. Profits for some come at the cost of environmental damage that affects us all.

Further, large corporate size demands an extremely advanced technology. It hinders the use of a lesser technology even where a lesser technology is logically appropriate. The less-developed nations of the world are not able, in many cases, to take advantage of high-technology production. They have neither the financial capital to buy these high technology capital goods nor the expertise to use them. Yet too often, in the pursuit of maximum profits, this technology is thrust upon them to the detriment of both their economic and social development. They would be infinitely better off were they able to grow more slowly at a rate more in keeping with their overall needs and capabilities, and in ways less destructive to their natural resources. Yet, they are required to choose the high technology or to remain as they are.

Lastly, large corporate size aggravates the already too high level of alienation that people suffer. A large-sized firm produces activity which is beyond a human scale, that level at which most humans can deal comfortably. It is not possible to cope with this heightened level of activity without higher levels of alienation.

The modern corporation is not a necessary form. It causes great problems and has great costs. They hinder competition. They have great governmental and social power. Their form should be modified or eliminated.

8   ECONOMIC SYSTEMS

A political economy is based on a theoretical economic model. It is necessary to look at the political economy model as well as the economic one. Even though there can be significant differences between theory and reality, it is still reasonable to expect that the resulting political economy will be at least somewhat in line with its model.

In Economic Organizations and Social Systems, Dr. Solo attends to the inevitable political ingredient and his models are realistic. He considers existing political economies so that his theoretical political economic systems and probable ramifications, both favorable and unfavorable, which most likely would follow from the application of each system, are practical ones. These ramifications are derived from models using a methodology that is rigidly objective. Further, the application of his methodology is rigorously logical and as practical as theory can be. He shows that a decentralized economy, one where most or all economic decisions are made at the individual level, will have problems at the macro level because of the way individuals make economic decisions.

The reason for this is a logical one. Individuals operate in their own self-interests ignoring negative externalities even when known. The interests of the whole economy are ignored, and existing problems are compounded. In a centralized economy, one where most decisions are made by a body chosen democratically or otherwise, that has effective control over individuals, decisions are supposed to be made in the interests of the economy as a whole. While this approach theoretically eliminates many macroeconomic problems, it compounds microeconomic ones. This approach reduces the status of the individual and freedom. The benefits that result from one system's approach create difficulties that are minimized in the other. Solo's is a thoroughgoing objective one.

Comparative Economic Systems approaches the problem from a

similar perspective, but the emphasis is different. Dr. Carson describes the various economic systems though not as *pure* systems. Carson's approach is geared towards real systems. Like Solo, Carson doesn't ignore the political. His purpose is "to derive 'a spectrum of economic systems,' to shed light on the differences and similarities between economics that the capitalist-socialist dichotomy tends to blur." Ideological issues need to be defused. He does so, but only enough to shed light on the differences and similarities. His main interest is in the economic model though he does not seem to be concerned about the theoretical limitations of *pure* systems. He mostly succeeds in his approach to considering primarily political economic theory as opposed to existing political economies.

A Theory of Economic Systems takes a more radical tack. Dr. Gottlieb seeks out the nature of historical economic systems. He attempts to uncover some of the historical reasons why existing economic systems developed as they did. His basic concerns are "(1) treatment of change in culture, institutions and technology; (2) ways in which separate economic systems may be drawn into meaningful multi-national gestalts or orders; and (3) problems of system classification." Though he doesn't analyze theoretical economic systems per se, he does show how they economic systems developed historically. Neither does he does not ignore the political. He is concerned with "functions of the state in the economy."

Capitalism or Worker Control?: An Ethical and Economic Appraisal is also concerned with models of the two major economic systems, but from a totally different perspective. Dr. Schweickart raises "the normative question, what socioeconomic structure best accords with current capabilities and a certain set of widely shared values?"

Schweickart looks at the criteria of efficiency and growth. He questions whether capitalism is efficient. He questions what *growth* means and whether it is desirable. He speaks of feasibility. His primary concern is to show that his socialist model is superior to existing economies.

Analysts attempt to objectively describe what is. They often don't succeed. If analysis is to be objective, it requires that the analysts rid themselves of their culture's ideological baggage. They seldom have.

It is a mistake to adopt an economic system under a mistaken impression that the subjective analysis is an objective one. Few presentations by advocates are value free. They often are laden with mistaken ideology. Much of their analysis, when done at all, is done against a predetermined and unanalyzed standard. The performance criteria used in the analysis must themselves be analyzed. They seldom are.

The performance of economic systems must be evaluated "in terms of a number of criteria or 'success indicators,'" a list of goals that must be reached or approximated if that system is to be highly evaluated.

Balassa "distinguishes and analyzes five success indicators: static efficiency, dynamic efficiency, growth, consumer satisfaction, and income distribution." Most analysts agree though some add others, among which are composition of output, stability, adaptability to change, allocation and the position of the individual within a system. Depending on the analyst, some of these criteria may differ or overlap, but in general, these are the ones most used.

The criteria themselves, however, all need to be analyzed before they can be accepted. This is particularly true of economic efficiency. After all, the result of an efficient economic system is said to be economic growth. For some, this is the exclusive, or almost exclusive, criterion.

Irrespective of any other differences there might be, most analysts compare the results achieved by an economic system with the results proponents of say should be obtained. They maintain that this is adequate because it is not their place to choose the goals for any economic system. They should only observe whether the goals selected have been achieved. The assumption is that if its goals have been reached or approximated, that economic system is relatively successful

Static efficiency: The concept of [static] efficiency refers to the effectiveness with which a system utilizes its available resources at a particular point in time." It "requires an economic system to be operating on its production possibilities frontier curve."

Though static efficiency is an important consideration in evaluating an economic system, it is not a sufficient one. Other criteria also must be met. Further, the claim that a system that achieves a high level of static efficiency is desirable needs defending. It is necessary to consider the costs of achieving a high level of static efficiency.

Dynamic efficiency: This term "refers to the ability of an economic system to enhance its capacity to produce goods and services over time without an increase in capital and labor inputs." Dynamic efficiency extends the production possibilities frontier curve outward to the right through innovation and/or invention. Examples are the discovery of crop rotation, the application of the bronze casting technique to iron, the specialized techniques of the *pin factory*, etc.

It was this about capitalism that so enthralled Joseph Schumpeter. Only capitalism, he said, could so improve the living conditions of the working class. "The capitalist achievement does not typically consist in providing more silk stockings for queens but in bringing them within the reach of factory girls in return for steadily decreasing amounts of effort."

Again, this criterion is not sufficient. There will always be other factors involved. Further, dynamic efficiency is not a necessary condition. It is possible for an economic system to make marginal improvements in other areas such that the results obtained are superior to those that a more dynamically efficient economic system might obtain.

In underdeveloped economies, dynamic efficiency is highly desirable, if not absolutely necessary. In some underdeveloped countries even if economic and social activity is as statically efficient as possible, there are still too few goods and services being produced for even simple survival. It is necessary in such cases to seek an expansion of the production possibilities frontier curve. Dynamic efficiency can be absolutely necessary. That a high level of it is essential in such a setting does not, however, make it essential in an already highly developed economy. Such a claim needs a defense.

Whether dynamic efficiency is ever desirable in a fully developed economy, and if so under what conditions, is a question that must be considered but seldom is. For an economic system to achieve dynamic efficiency, costs must be paid. One such cost is structural upheaval. Growth, especially rapid growth, can cause unforeseen and sometimes disastrous changes in the social and political fabric as well as in the economy. Before a society decides to encourage a dynamically efficient economic system, these costs should be evaluated relative to the benefits obtained. This is seldom done.

Growth: This is "a sustained upward movement in the aggregate level of output (or output per person)." Economic growth is not the same as dynamic efficiency, though it is easy to confuse the two because dynamic efficiency results in increased economic output.

Economic growth can come about in several ways or combination of them. First, it can be a result of intensive economic activity. Intensive growth is "increases in factor productivity," a better way of doing something without increasing the amount of resources consumed. Intensive growth is similar to dynamic efficiency. It is just a different definition.

Economic growth also can be achieved through extensive economic activity, "by expanding the amount of labor [or another factor] but using that labor [or other factor] at a constant rate of effectiveness." In a fully developed economy, however, "these extra inputs are likely to incur sacrifices in the forms of time not previously allocated to production and goods previously allocated to current consumption." When a high level of static efficiency exists, extensive growth has as its opportunity cost either decreased leisure or decreased consumption, or some combination thereof. While this phenomenon might be called economic growth, it can hardly be referred to as overall growth since sacrifices equal to the economic growth must be incurred in other areas.

Lastly, economic growth can result from "an outward shift in the production possibilities frontier curve caused by an increase in available resources." This is different than intensive growth which expands the production possibilities frontier curve without an increase in resources.

These different ways of expanding production cause some analysts to become confused. It is said that there is economic growth whenever the quantity produced increases. But this is not necessarily true, for several reasons.

First, increased production can come about because of an increase in static efficiency. *Ceteris paribus*, this is undoubtedly desirable, but it is not economic growth as defined by the economic systems analyst. It is static efficiency.

Second, increased production can come about through extensive growth. While such increased production may be necessary because of exigent circumstances, it still is not what is meant when it is said that economic growth is desirable.

Third, increased production can come about through intensive growth. This increased production can be a large benefit to society though it isn't always.

Lastly, increased production can come about because of an increase in resources. If this is growth, it needs a defense.

Too often, the aforementioned types of increased production are collapsed into one. The first two situations are not economic growth. Of the last two, only one, that which results from an increase in resources, can be, unless dynamic efficiency is to be lost as a concept. It cannot be both economic growth and a cause of economic growth.

Consumer satisfaction: This is achieved when, subject to their available resources, individuals are able to maximize their utility, "the ability of a good to satisfy a want" and to have the freedom such that there is "correspondence of production targets to individual preferences; correspondence of actual saving ratio to the saving ratio desired by individuals; (and) correspondence of actual work performed to individuals' preference for work versus leisure."

While the indicators static efficiency, dynamic efficiency, and growth are value-free, some say that the indicator consumer satisfaction, in deciding what should be produced to create a high level of consumer satisfaction, introduces a subjective element. Consumer sovereignty is a different question. Should consumers decide for themselves what they want produced, or should someone else decide for them? It is the value which is placed upon the criterion that is subjective, not the criterion itself. Consumer sovereignty must be among the criteria if the concept of freedom is to mean anything.

Income distribution: This is how an economic system determines for whom products and services are to be produced. Whatever decision is arrived at or whatever decision-making process is used, the final determination will seldom satisfy everyone. The issue of equitable economic distribution is frequently fought over, particularly outside of economics.

The capitalist says that there is an adequate answer to this question, that each factor of production receives its marginal physical product, the change in revenue that results from the increase in total product when an additional unit in a factor is added to a production process that is already in existence. The concept appears equitable, but it seldom is. There is no way in which the 'marginal productivity' of any factor can be determined independently of the contribution of other factors. The most powerful factor usually receives *more* of its marginal physical product than a weaker one does. The prior distribution of resources also affects current distribution of income. If the prior distribution was not equitable, it is unlikely that the current distribution will be either.

Composition of output: This is the portion of the gross national product that each sector of the economy receives. It is important to consider the amount of production relegated to the private sector as opposed to the public sector, to investment as opposed to military programs, etc. This criterion differs from distribution of income in that it considers collective consumption, those sectors of the economy usually considered by national income accounting which is not considered when referring to income distribution.

Economic stability: This is the absence of "the fluctuations upward and downward in the overall level of [economic] activity." This criterion is a concern of the economic public policy of the United States. It strives for slow-but-steady economic growth, high employment, and stable prices.

Adaptability to change: This is a "well adjusted mechanisms in the system that help it adjust to changing circumstances without endangering the basic working of the system. Without these mechanisms, the economy will either become stagnant within an obsolete institutional framework or be hit by abrupt changes of a revolutionary character." It is necessary for an economic system to allow for both dynamic change, innovation and invention, and static change, marginal improvements in the existing system if frequent contradictions in the system are to be avoided. Without the ability to allow for change, an economic system will confront situations where the new is in severe conflict with the old.

An example of failure to adequately allow for change is the

tendency of existing social structures to remain as they are even when changes are being made within them. Sometimes the need for change is so great that it is obvious to everybody but to those who have systemic advantages and then want those advantages to be *grandfathered-in.* No one new will be allowed to have these advantages, but those who already possess them will not surrender them even though they might be causing great harm.

It is not realistic to expect a system to allow for changes. As has already been shown, Adam Smith, John Locke, and Paul Sweezy, among others, have told us that the highest purpose of the state and of the economic system it controls is the protection of the interests of those who are in charge and who thereby benefit from the system. Further, neither a political nor an economic system can make provision for changes that are contrary to its basic characteristics and goals. It is not rational to expect that too much change will be allowed for.

It is desirable that a system, economic or otherwise, protect itself from destruction by allowing for marginal change. The benefits gained and the costs avoided by allowing for potential changes are cheap at half the price. If this is all that is meant by adaptability to change, it doesn't mean much.

The position of the individual within the system: "Individual security and satisfaction compromise more than merely freedom from want and fear, although these are important. They include freedom to do things, to resist things, to think and say things, even to make a fool of one's self." The criterion of consumer sovereignty usually is advocated because the advocate favors economic freedom. The position of the individual in the system goes beyond economic freedom. It includes political freedom as well.

This criterion is more concerned with political economy than with pure economics. However, many rightfully consider it the most singularly important of all the criteria by which an economic system is judged. If one cannot have political freedom, great economic freedoms are without meaning.

The political freedom of the individual is of overriding importance. Any system that does not respect the political and social rights of the individual or have them as its immediate objective should be automatically rejected out-of-hand.

The normal criteria for judging an economic system are inadequate since several of them are not well understood even by the economic systems analysts themselves. Capitalism is advocated as a superior system because it is efficient and is capable of a high level of economic growth. Both of these claims are debatable, and if they are to be used as criteria, they must first be proven. More is needed than a concept of technical efficiency and unrestrained growth that doesn't consider all the costs of growth. Using these criteria alone leads to failure to ask the correct questions.

In addition to analyzing theoretical economic systems, it is necessary to analyze existing economic systems. After all, they exist in the world. It is an important analysis to do. What needs to be done first, however, is to analyze the economic theory in light of its consistency with itself, with overall economic theory, and with the ends of a rational society. The goal in all of this is to improve the human condition.

Further, an economic system cannot be analyzed in an apolitical vacuum. An understanding of the relationship between the economic system and the political system is essential. Still further, it must be remembered that both government and economy contain coercive elements.

An evaluation of an economic system must consider the costs and benefits of what the system does irrespective of the criteria used to judge or measure it. Each of the criteria have costs which must be paid in return for any benefits derived. These criteria must be considered both individually and in comparison to each other.

Static efficiency can have costs, such as alienation, that are much too high to pay. Growth and dynamic efficiency are often confused with one another. Consumer satisfaction and consumer sovereignty are not the same thing. Consumption is the end of all economic activity, not efficiency of whatever kind. Equitable income distribution cannot be ignored. If labor is the source of all socially created value, it can be argued that labor should receive all socially created value. Lastly, the position of the individual in both the economic system and society at large is of paramount importance. At least one of the purposes of the collective is to enhance the status of the individual. The human is a social creature. It gathers into groups in order to create opportunities for individuals to better themselves. An institutionalized social system, economic or otherwise, has no other legitimate purpose.

An economic system is influenced by everything.

9   SYNOPSIS of CAPITALISM

Capitalism has never been a static system. It has always been dynamic. The system is not now what it once was. It has changed as it has developed. Its goal, however, has always been the same, the accumulation of great private wealth for the purpose of protecting and extending that great wealth. This is accomplished by using that wealth as a means of power both over production and over others.

Historically, capitalism began with the struggle of the individual to obtain power based upon the emerging idea that the individual was absolute. This idea was incorporated into the theory of the *Invisible Hand.* It was and is claimed that the application of this theory would produce the best society. It would best enable all to survive in the best possible condition. But, it hasn't.

The *standard* model of capitalism is offered as support for this claim. It is inadequate. Capitalism is not efficient in any sense of the word. It is not economically efficient. Pareto Optimality does not obtain even with the aid of government. Neither is it technically efficient. Almost all firms are price-makers.

Further, the results of the system are in conflict with its ideology. The ideology promises much for all, but the system has created a structure wherein many are impoverished or worse.

Capitalism is confused with competition even though they are far from being the same things. Capitalism subverts its model whenever necessary.

The economic system supposedly chosen by society, one based on perfect competition, is not the one that society has received. Goods are produced, by both the private and the public sector, in isolation; mainstream consumer behavior theory is almost completely incorrect; uninformed markets are everywhere; few, aside from the producers, have complete or adequate information; little behavior in this system can meaningfully be called rational.

Production in this *free market* is almost totally dominated by price-making firms facing downward-sloping demand curves resulting in innumerous market imperfections. Besides the non-production of public goods, there are many negative externalities and criminal underproduction. Rather than promoting benign competition, it creates noxious competition. It results in the micro sector receiving benefits for creating costs for which the macro sector becomes responsible.

Each firm seeks to control the price of its product and, hence, over the size of its profit. Competition is not a standard towards which the capitalist voluntarily moves. Quite the contrary. It is something the capitalist abhors. Business people don't want competition. They want market control.

The market is antisocial. It is coercive. It prohibits cooperation. It pits one against all. The market is not objective. It is subjective. The prices generated by the market do not accurately reflect costs and values. Neither is it efficient or cost-free. The market ignores much that it should not. It generates negative externalities much greater than normally thought. The market claims a lot, but it doesn't consider what it needs to if its claims are to be realized.

This is done in the pursuit of profit, a result which requires a legitimate justification. It has never been forthcoming. Some economic profit can be socially beneficial when it is fairly earned. Most isn't.

Nor does labor have the freedom to contract. Only capital, private property, has that freedom, and it is not neutral. It exists for, and is protected by, somebody.

Prices take on an added definition. They are what must be paid to release the coercive power created by the institution of private property. The *Invisible Hand* isn't so invisible. Most firms operate without regard to ethics or anything else that is not a direct cost to the firm.

Using great supplies of natural resources to increase economic growth produces even more disaster. Nature is no longer self-healing. Its wounds are too severe. Capitalism does not make any distinction between the way prices are determined for renewable as opposed to non-renewable resources.

Though capitalism has increased many aspects of our standard of living, it has greatly reduced others. Some of these costs can never be repaid. There are significant mental and emotional externalities. Noxious competition replaces rational self-interest. That the interest of the other can also be mine is seldom acknowledged.

There is no minimum standard of distributional justice. Poverty is epidemic. Just as most wars are financed through deficit spending because few will tolerate present taxation to pay for them, few pay to eliminate poverty. People believe against all evidence that capitalism will feed everyone if only each will take advantage of the opportunities presented.

Neither are capitalists consistent in stating the purpose of government. Some say that government is necessary to provide public goods. Others say that government should serve as the impartial arbiter of justice. Still others, recognizing the impossibility of impartiality, propose that government should control the excesses of the markets. They are opposed by libertarians who propose the pursuit of unfettered capitalism as everyone's unconditional right.

Much of the industrial advance claimed to have been generated by capitalism was fueled by limited liability. Many potential investors did not invest because they feared exposure to unlimited liability. Limited liability alleviated this fear.

With industrial advance came great industrial and financial

concentration. Propaganda falsely claimed that such great concentration was necessary if economies of scale were to be realized, if consumers were to receive more products at lower prices. Large profits were the reason for it.

The capitalists themselves even chose government interference and antitrust regulation as preferable to unfettered libertarian competition. They knew that they could control the regulation through the financing of selected politicians. A *laissez faire* government doesn't exist because it can't.

The result was that society incurred large costs while the oligopolistic industries obtained the large share of the benefits.

Accepting these results is hard for people. They want to believe that they are well-informed and rational and that they operate in their self-interests. The reality of capitalism is in conflict with its ideology. The system doesn't do what it says it is going to do. It is not socially efficient.

10   QUESTIONS and ANSWERS

What is being analyzed? What is the capitalists' definition of capitalism? No one wants to define it. A well explicated definition of capitalism conflicts with the model of perfect competition which touts it as a superior market structure.

The adherents leave the definition confused. It is only through a careful collecting of selected bits and pieces of the capitalist concept that the big picture can be painted. If the definition is clearly stated, the conflict becomes obvious. The model says it objectively justifies what is. It doesn't. The model can't justify actual economic activity.

Leaving everything vague allows each part to be shifted around to explain or justify whatever else needs to be explained or justified even if that explanation might contradict another part of the system. It is less likely that the contradictions will be seen. The model is merely a pedagogical device, and not a very good one at that. It is confusing and misleading. These are not traits one normally attributes to an adequate pedagogical device.

The model doesn't reflect what capitalists say capitalism is or what they want to accomplish. One claimed justification is that it can serve as a *standard* by which we measure market imperfections. It doesn't do this. It is used to justify market imperfections themselves.

Keynes was correct when he said capitalism is an inherently unstable economic system. A model or system must be rational. It cannot have contradictory assumptions or results that contradict its purpose. This is not acceptable.

"Does capitalism justify itself when measured against its own criteria?" Mainstream economists agree that the system is to promote the best society. They claim that this is accomplished via the *Invisible Hand*. The *Invisible Hand*, however, is only an ideology. It is believed, but seldom understood, and never adequately defended. The theory hasn't worked in the real world. Yet, the theory is still held.

Many financial economists have advocated that "banks [be] required to maintain 100 percent reserves against demand deposits [checking accounts]." Improvements in banking efficiency would be dramatic. This is opposed by most bankers. Their profitability would be reduced drastically "because they would no longer be able to create money. Therefore, despite its benefits, the system is never likely to be adopted."

Further examples of corporations acting in their own self-interest abound. General Motors, General Electric, General Dynamics, General Aniline and Film. Were it not for Reserve Mining, Ford Motor Company, and A. H. Robins, one might say that our economy suffers from a *General* problem. These are not isolated instances nor are they anecdotal. This behavior has become commonplace. So much for the *Invisible Hand*. It fails to lead to a better society. It often leads to an inferior one.

A few hundred years ago when the market system first began to establish itself, it appeared that the *Invisible Hand* was actually *visible*. Life for the many was improved for some time under capitalism. However, conditions were such that any accomplishment would have been a material improvement.

If the *Invisible Hand* was the reason why capitalism was accepted and that reason is wrong, then either a new and better reason must be provided or a different system must be offered for consideration. Capitalism is a failed ideology, a rationalization designed to defend the status quo. It misleads even students of the system. Capitalism has never produced the best society.

In much of the world, capitalism does not even provide for survival, but for exploitation. The United States is only about 6 percent of the Earth's population yet it consumes about one-third of the Earth's production and natural resources. It will be assumed that the populations of Europe, Russia and China are about the same percentage and that they each consume about the same as do the people of the United States. If these *for-the-sake-of-argument* assumptions were real, one-quarter of the world's population would be consuming one-third more than everything. The remaining three-quarters would have nothing to consume. Truth is not so different. Much of the world lives in poverty, and many live in absolute poverty. They are starving.

As population increases, technology advances, and expectations rise, the demand upon the nonrenewable, limited, resources increases. This mode of growth cannot continue. Simple survival is becoming less probable for many.

Yet, there are constant calls for further growth. Every nation has, as part of its economic public policy, a goal of continued economic growth. No one asks where that growth will come from or at whose expense it will be enjoyed. They just want it even if that growth is not possible for all. If some are to have it, it must be at the expense of others.

Yet, capitalism continues its Topsy-like growth, oblivious to those costs because its economic calculus doesn't allow for the inclusion of evidence that would show its activities to be the chimeras of rationality that they are. Environmental problems will always with us. Nature has its tolerances beyond which it cannot be pushed. Within these tolerances, nature is self-healing. Waste matter is a natural by-product of living. As long as the quantity of that by-product is not larger than the amount nature can recycle, there will not be any pollution.

A reason why capitalism was initially as successful as it was is that nature was relatively healthy at the beginning of the capitalist era, and capitalism itself was not too extended. Nature was able to withstand the initial onslaught of a great amount of pollution. Even though it was unable to recycle all of it, it at least was able to survive with it. There were places to hide it. Now, we have neither a healthy environment nor a place to hide our ever-increasing quantity of waste products.

Negative externalities are a result of the logic of the capitalist productive process. It puts a price on only those things that it must. It values the environment only when it is forced by something or someone external to the economic system to put a price on it. Sizable fines and penalties would imposes empirical limiting operating condition upon the capitalist when making economic decisions about the environment.

If a thing does not have a price or if that price can somehow be ignored, it is only logical that it should be ignored. Capitalism's end is profit maximization. Negative externalities are costs that lessens profit. Negative externalities are ignored. Under capitalism, negative externalities are not exceptions. They are the rule.

It is irrational to determine the costs of renewable and non-renewable resources in the same way. The former are replaceable. The latter are not. Yet, the market does not distinguish between them. As our nonrenewable natural resources are used up, production becomes increasingly more difficult and more costly.

Further, non-renewable resources are our biological capital, but capitalism treats them as income. A business that treats its capital as income will soon go out of business. In this instance, *going out of business* means the death of us. That is just too high a cost to ignore.

Free goods, goods that are both abundant and desired, clean air and water, are gone. In a large part of the world, they are no longer clean. Growth has eliminated them. They aren't free goods any longer. It is now necessary to pay for them.

These are problems that come with increased production. Even as our material possessions increases, our material standard of living decreases. This is not a desirable result.

Even if all the physical negatives, garbage pollution, noise pollution, people profusion, itself a pollution, are ignored, an increase in material welfare still doesn't necessarily bring an increase in the standard of living. There is more to be considered. An increasing Gross National Product says that we are *better off*. Besides these *disproducts*, these negative externalities that the GNP doesn't consider, it still omits much: leisure and other human costs, particularly the physical and mental strain, the *alienation*, that are associated with most labor jobs. Capitalism cannot exist without labor. Capitalism exacerbates workers' alienation. Thus, alienation of the unpropertied is inevitable. This is a cost. Yet, alienation is not included in the system's economic calculus.

Capitalism argues that alienation is included because the worker considers its cost in his cost-benefit analysis and is reimbursed for it in the form of higher wages. This is not the case. Labor is not free to contract. To survive, labor must accept the accompanying alienation without compensation.

Alienation from the labor process and from the product of one's labor is not the only form of alienation. Each is also alienated from the other. Humans are social creatures. They cannot find fulfillment in any but a social setting. Capitalism and the market, however, create noxious competition, a setting where there is a war of each against all. It prohibits cooperation as irrational. It ignores the interest of the other even when the interest of the other is mine. Yet, competition is advocated as a reason why capitalism should be embraced.

Capitalists say that they are efficient. They are not. Without government, capitalism leaves society without public goods. Further, many of them are produced in a high degree of isolation. Capitalism is not technically efficient either since almost all its firms produce inside the production possibility frontier curve. Neither is capitalism socially efficient. It doesn't do what it says it will do. Capitalism fails on all of counts.

Neither does capitalism fulfill "the minimum standard of distributional justice." Much of this problem has been caused by an underutilization of resources. Firms are price-makers . The large number of price-makers has come about because of corporations, those artificial creations of the state, which have become so large that they have developed great market power. Corporations have become virtually uncontrollable even by the state which created them.

The present corporate form does not fit society's needs. It is antithetical to those needs allowing corporations to further their self-interest. Neither is the market what it claims to be.

Capitalism has provided much that has been beneficial and can continue to be so if the system can be modified. Some desirable parts might be retained in a new and different system. However, few believe that it can be so modified. Too many vested interests in modern capitalism have been grandfathered in becoming impenetrable fortresses of power.

What is any given society really trying to accomplish? Each society has certain goals it wishes to achieve. The goals must be plausible. They must be possible. They must be sincere. They still must meet certain criteria if they are to be taken seriously. They must not be mere propaganda. A society that acts contrary to its goals must be judged harshly.

Is what a society is trying to accomplish what should be accomplished? A society should seek to promote the individual and the individual's place in that society. It should create and further opportunities for individuals to become better people and to lead more-human lives. A more human life involves doing what is proper for a person advancing towards self-sufficiency and happiness. Society should help the individual take advantage of such opportunities. Society exists for the purpose of people not the other way around.

That much is left to question here. What is *better*? What is *more human*? What is *proper*? What is the *purpose* of the individual? What is the *purpose* of people? Are those *purposes* different?. These questions must be dealt with rationally, "for grasp of a reasoned conclusion is the primary condition of knowledge," and it is knowledge that we seek.

The human is a conscious, reasoning being for whom "the basic means of survival is reason." "If one turns against thought, the struggle can only succeed by thought. The destruction of thought always remains itself still thought ... The fate of thought is the destiny of our humanity." Whatever society's goals might be, they must be rational and must promote the human condition. A society should do what is rational. If it is not, then it is doesn't do what it should be.

Are society's underlying assumptions rational, not contradictory nor antagonistic to themselves or one another, in theory or in practice? Are they consistent with furthering the human condition? The must be both internally logically consistent, correct and externally logically consistent. It is necessary that every argument and its premises be consistent with every other argument and premise. Each argument must be externally logically consistent with every other one. If they are not, society will surely be troubled.

Is society's ideology consistent with its actual construction? Every society has an ideology that serves as its justification, but it is necessary that that ideology be consistent with the society's actual construction.

Ideology develops in order to serve one or another group's self-interest usually at the expense of some other groups' interests. Beliefs in a patriarchal family, the natural inferiority of slaves, the divine right of kings are typical examples of ideologies which were inconsistent with the best interests of other members of the society promoting such ideologies. Ideology always supports the interests of the strongest class against the interests of the weakest ones. This is the root of class struggle.

The *expert* analyst must recognize that societies have ideologies. The social or political analyst must understand the ideologies of the societies they study.

What kind of a political system should a society adopt in order to accomplish its goals? This question is a subjective one, but there are some logical answers.

The political system, like the social system, must be empirically possible. A society's political system should rationally implement the goals of that society consistent with both that society's goals and its assumptions. Further, the political system must allow for as much input as possible from as many people as possible. It will be as close to a direct democracy as possible. People need to choose for themselves.

Fascism is the antithesis of such a system. Subordinating the individual to the whole is the antithesis of direct democracy. If self-determination is a legitimate human goal, then to be ruled by others, no matter how well intentioned, is to be less than alive. If it is correct that individuals form societies so that each individual might improve her or his condition, then fascism is not a rational social system. While certain aspects of an individual's condition might be enhanced by a fascist system, other aspects are sacrificed, aspects that are too high a cost to pay for the achievements of others.

Until recently, even to approximate a condition of direct democracy was thought to be physically impossible because of the large numbers of people that would have to be accommodated. With modern technology, it is becoming more and more feasible every day, if it isn't feasible already.

A *bourgeois democracy* is designed to protect the interests of the propertied class, a system that only has the appearances of democracy, not the actualities.

A meaningful democracy is necessary if there is to be a free society irrespective of the resistance of those who benefit from the existing property relations. A meaningful democracy does not mean the rule of the majority over the minority.

The present economic system is inadequate. The system is a failure for the many, most of whom bear unconscionably high burdens. The political apparatus is not actually a democracy but only a semblance of one. Those who disproportionately receive a much greater share of the system's benefits control the political apparatus for their continued benefit.

The Soviet experience is an example of how *leaders* do what they do and how they develop into a class that benefit from it. Their type of society an unacceptable alternative. Society's end is the self-sufficiency and happiness of individuals.

What kind of an economic system should a society adopt in order to accomplish its goals? The economic system must be possible. It should be designed to rationally address those social and other goals that can be accomplished or whose accomplishment can be aided by an economic system.

The analysis of economic systems cannot be done in a vacuum. All economic activity takes place against a social and political backdrop. It is necessary to consider the above questions. They are important. An economic system must be consistent with basic economic theory. Economics is, after all, economics Such incompatibility is grounds for immediate rejection.

Capitalism must be considered against a social and political backdrop. The stated goals of capitalism are at least acceptable. In some respects, they are even laudable. Capitalism seeks an adequate condition of material welfare for everyone such that each will be able to develop his or her human potential to the highest degree possible. Granted, the system may emphasize material welfare to the detriment of other kinds of development, but the claim is that it is an effort to improve the human condition. This goal seems to agree with rational human ends.

The actual results of capitalism, however, differ substantially from its stated goals. Capitalism's actual goal, to accumulate wealth and power, contradicts its stated goal and ideology.

The political system usually associated with it has held true to the tenet that the highest purpose of the state is to protect the interests of the ruling class. It cannot legitimately be claimed that it is democratic. The political system functions to subvert the stated goals of society.

Neither is capitalism rational as an economic system. It acts to subvert any rational understanding of cost.

Does capitalism *want* efficiency? Capitalism is not efficient in any sense of the word.

Capitalism is not economically efficient. All costs must be considered, yet the capitalist producer will do anything to externalize costs in order to increase the firm's profits. Such a system is not efficient.

Capitalism is not technically efficient either. Capitalist firms are price-makers. This allows the individual firm to face a downward sloping demand curve. Hardly any firm produces on its production possibilities frontier curve. Production almost always occurs inside the curve.

Capitalism fares even worse when measured for social efficiency. There are numerous people in capitalist nations, even in the U.S., who live substantially sub-par lives, economically and otherwise.

To be considered efficient, an economic system must be economically efficient. To be economically efficient, it must consider all costs. The system must also be technically efficient. It must produce on the production possibilities frontier curve. To be socially efficient, it must do what it should do and what it says it will do. Capitalism fails miserably in all these areas. Capitalism is inefficient.

Is the growth that capitalism seeks desirable? There are three possible sources of economic growth, four if it is assumed that production is not already taking place on the production possibilities frontier curve. There is extensive growth, intensive growth, which is the same thing as dynamic efficiency; and growth which results from an increase in resources. Each is different and may or may not be desirable or necessary under different circumstances.

Extensive growth can only occur when the production possibilities frontier curve is shifted outward to the right by the application of resources that were previously idle. More resources must be added; particularly labor. The opportunity cost for this increased labor is almost always foregone leisure. This price is usually paid only in an emergency such as a war or a natural disaster. Extensive growth for growth's sake is seldom desirable.

Intensive growth is dynamic efficiency. If the growth occurs as the result of a procedural breakthrough such as the discovery of crop rotation, the application of the casting technique from bronze to iron, etc., it can be cost-free, and additional benefits truly result. If, however, intensive growth is a result of a new procedure that also includes a more intense use of labor, e.g., Taylorism, costs can outweigh benefits. A more intense use of labor brings human costs. Working harder is the same as worker longer. Sometimes, intensive growth is the same as extensive growth. Either is desirable only when necessary due to emergencies. If, however, techniques are found that make a process more dynamically efficient without an accompanying human cost, they are to be sought.

Gaining additional resources can be a desirable type of growth. The difficulty is that in the finite world with its expanding population possession of additional resources usually comes by taking them from someone else.

Lastly, seldom are all costs considered particularly when the additional resources are non-renewable natural ones. There is a difference in kind when the costs of renewable resources are compared to non-renewable resources. By definition, non-renewable resources are finite. They cannot be replaced. Renewable resources can be. Yet, capitalism usually measures both as if they were the same.

If the additional resources necessary for growth are not obtained by taking them from others and all costs are paid, the growth that results is probably desirable. But, the economic growth of one economy is not desirable if it is achieved at the expense of another. Economic growth attained in that way is not economic growth.

When called upon to do so, the practical instantiations of capitalism have usually been able to achieve extensive growth. Historically, they have been able to expand production when emergencies have arisen. For instance, the U.S. industrial machine rose to the productive task of World War II and the subsequent rebuilding of much of Europe.

Real-world capitalism has been adept at achieving intensive growth. Much of it, however, has had costs that were not duly considered. Capitalism may have introduced new production techniques which have improved one aspect of the human condition, but it has also instituted much that has imposed costs that far outweigh the benefits. Much of this latter type of growth has been the result of working harder.

Another problem is how most capitalistic nations has attained *true* economic growth, possession of additional resources. After a country reaches a certain maturity, much of its growth has come through taking resources from others or not paying the full costs to nature. This is not the behavior expected from societies that refer to themselves as *just* societies.

The reasons why capitalism has so many failures are that its assumptions are contradictory or unreasonable.

A society cannot promote harmony and the self-sufficiency and happiness of the individual if each individual is set off against others. Yet, this is what capitalism does. The market is basically anti-social. Maybe, it can't be any other way.

Social costs which accompany a market economy must be considered. Competition is supposed to bring us our daily bread and brew in an efficient manner. Not only does it fail to do so, it makes conditions worse. Adam Smith described benign competition. Most competition today is non-price competition, advertising. We know the difference between advertising that informs and advertising that appeals to the base. Most advertising is noxious. This is not conducive to producing the *best* society. Yet, it is encouraged by the system itself. Today, competition is noxious competition. It destroys rather than creates.

There are problems with the system's institutions. Today's institutions support today's wealth and power, but not the system's stated goals. They are not neutral. They are not eternal. They can and do die. They can be changed or eliminated. This is not *capitalism revisionism*, but corrections of errors.

Neither is gradual change the intention, but to make a way to improve a system already in place which is functioning in a way contrary to the way it is intended to function in the hope that something practical will come of it. Perhaps, it won't be of any use. Maybe, change must be abrupt and revolutionary. But perhaps, some significant change can be brought about rationally through a new public political-economic debate.

Economic analysts wish to move society toward where it says it wants to go by developing better theory and exploring practical possibilities. What can be done to make the existing system more viable?

Economic profit can be acceptable if it is earned in a socially beneficial manner. The economic system of a society is not the social order. It is but a part of it. If economic profits are being earned by a process that is not socially beneficial, particularly if that process is socially harmful, as opposed to being socially benign, then society should take steps to make such profits difficult, if not impossible, to obtain.

To justify economic profits, the profit must be made by including all production costs. The firm must internalize all costs including negative externalities that are known or can reasonably be expected to be internalized. Some negative externalities are so minimal that the cost of internalizing them is prohibitive. What is reasonable will be discovered in the process of working it out. Ways must be found for society to construct itself so that it would be natural for it to find those negative externalities rather than to hide them.

Economic profit should be a the reward to those whose efforts produced it, not those who did not put forth the effort. It should not be the result of exploitation. Under capitalism, *exploitation* is common. It is a payment to a factor of production less than the true value of that factor's marginal product.

Economic profit is now earned through market control. Thus, any degree of market control need to be justified. Granting of market control is the idea behind the granting of patents and copyrights. These grants by the state are intended to promote inventions, works of art, etc. which in turn are intended to promote the human condition. Some market control is the originator's reward. The originator should have a reasonable opportunity to earn reasonable rewards for that originality, and it is through this state-granted and state-protected monopoly that these rewards, in the form of economic profits, can be earned. Little other market control should be allowed unless a case for its existence can be made.

"An important factor in existing inequality, both of income and of power, is the gigantic corporation. The granting of rights which allows and promotes this inequality is one of the greatest sins of government against the free-enterprise system." Which is more important, the unlimited financial and industrial growth of a corporation or the free enterprise system? The two are mutually exclusive possibilities. If the free enterprise system is more important, then the power of the corporation must be delimited.

It is the state's gift of limited liability that has allowed corporations to become as large as they have. To be sure, the state receives social benefits from this gift, but limited liability is a gift of the state, nonetheless. It is the state, therefore, that has the right, indeed the duty, to delimit the private benefits that accrue to the recipient of that gift so that more is not given than society can afford to give.

Then, how much power should a corporation be given? The maximum size which can reasonably be argued for is the minimum efficient scale, "the level of output at which economies of scale are exhausted."

The privilege of limited liability should be revoked for any corporation that is larger than the minimum efficient scale. There isn't any social justification for a corporation being larger. The only purpose for such a large size is the private benefits that result. The results of such a maximum-size limitation would be almost instantaneous. Every corporation larger than the maximum size allowed would shrink to whatever maximum size was allowed almost immediately because without limited liability, corporate stock would drop in value drastically since the threat of suits under which total personal bankruptcy for individual investors could result would be a cost not many investors would bear voluntarily. Few corporate Watts would retain their Boultons for very long.

Large institutional investors currently control a very substantial portion of the available investment dollars. The large institutional investors, in particular, being obligated to operate as *prudent men*, would be forbidden, for all practical purposes to own shares in corporations that did not have limited liability. This change would not reduce investment, but it would make funds available to more and different sources.

Even at minimum efficient scale, an argument still can be made that a given firm is too large. There are large costs that are not incorporated into the firm's economic calculus, primarily workers' alienation. By reducing the firm to minimum efficient scale, the amount of alienation will be reduced, but the remaining alienation probably would still be substantial. Should a firm's size be reduced below the minimum efficient scale so that alienation can be reduced even further?

Some industries have decreasing long-run average cost curves that are relatively flat, as opposed to those industries where they are relatively steep. Those industries incur rather small increased costs if they operate below minimum efficient scale.

The cigarette industry's minimum efficient scale is 6.6 percent of total U.S. consumption. If each corporation that manufactured cigarettes were exactly the size necessary to maintain minimum efficient scale, there would be approximately 15 cigarette manufacturers. The four-firm concentration ratio now, however, is 81 percent. That means that four cigarette manufacturers produce 81 percent of the cigarettes. Knowing that there is no social justification for their manufacture in the first place, they can be reduced in size even below the minimum efficiency of scale at very little additional cost. The increase in cost for a cigarette manufacturer operating at one-third minimum efficiency of scale is only 2.2 percent. This means there could be approximately 45 firms instead of the eight that there are now with a cost of only 2.2 percent above the cost of minimum efficient scale. The result such size reduction would have upon price and profit would be minimal. For a small increase in operating costs, a significant amount of additional competition would result. This increased competition would cause consumer prices to decrease and economic profits to be reduced greatly, if not to disappear altogether. The market for cigarettes would then be as it should be under capitalism. It would provide the best possible product at the lowest possible price.

Such forced size limitation is justified. There aren't any social benefits that could justify the economic profits currently being received by the oligopolistic cigarette manufacturers.

The minimum efficient scale for a cement manufacturer is 1.7 percent of total U.S. consumption. The existing four-firm concentration ratio is 29 percent. This ratio can easily be reduced to 6.8 percent at little or no cost while obtaining increased social benefits. There could easily be approximately 59 cement manufacturers. Any further size reductions, however, would not be quite so desirable. Were a cement manufacturer to operate at one-third of minimum efficient scale, costs would increase 26 percent. This might be too high a cost to pay for the benefits that might result.

Since these favorable numbers do not hold in all industries, criteria would have to be established to address these problems. In some cases, the guidelines established ultimately could end up being quite arbitrary. In others, they would be well-founded and obvious.

In some industries, such as the cigarette industry, there might be still other factors involved. In that industry, the social costs of smoking need to be considered. Subsidizing the tobacco industry in light of what is known about the dangers of smoking is not consistent with rational social ends. That subsidization allows for great profits to be made while producing substantial negative externalities. Therefore, allowed size might be reduced even further than one-third of minimum efficient scale in that industry

Because of the differences in the slopes of the decreasing cost curves of the tobacco and cement industries and other social costs, firms in one of them might be allowed to retain their limited liability as long as they didn't exceed minimum efficient scale while firms in the other would not be allowed to exceed one-third minimum efficient scale without being forced to surrender it.

The actual industries and numbers aren't important. What is is there is a rational maximum size that a corporation should be allowed to reach and that society address the issue.

These changes in corporate size would not be cost-free. A new and large bureaucracy would be required. No sane person likes bureaucracies, but the cost and burdens of this new one would be substantially less than the corporate bureaucracies it would be replacing.

Another problem would be the power granted to this new bureaucracy would not be a little one. It would be a great and potentially dangerous power. Advocates of small government seldom advocate Small is Beautiful. They enjoy the power of *Oversized is Beautiful.* No one ever said it would be easy.

"Even if the much-advertised economies of gigantic financial combinations were real, sound policy would wisely sacrifice these economies to preservation of more economic freedom and equality." Exceeding human scale is another cost. Large-scale production produces effects with which individuals simply cannot deal, emotional pressures and the resulting alcoholism, drug abuse, physical abuse, suicide, divorce, etc. These costs must be dealt with, but never are.

The destruction of the environment's biological capital is another cost. The cost of a non-renewable resource is substantially different than that of a renewable resource. Yet, the market doesn't consider this difference. It treats them both the same way. As with other costs that the market ignores this cost must be considered in production decisions.

There might be industries where it would be thought it to be worth paying the social costs necessary to enjoy the benefits of their large scale production. So, be it.

There also might be industries that could not be made competitive no matter what was done. In such a case, "the state should face the necessity of actually taking over, owning and managing directly all industries in which it is impossible to maintain effectively competitive condition."

Such governmental involvement already is accepted when the industry is a natural monopoly, "a market situation in which the average costs of production continually decline with increased output." Local public utilities are examples that approximate these conditions. Government regulation of public utilities is seldom fought-over in capitalism. It is not much of a step to say that government should involve itself actively in those industries where effectively competitive conditions cannot be maintained or where large-scale production, production at minimum efficiency of scale, is deemed to be socially desirable. Anticipating the *slippery-slope* argument of the critics, no one ever said it would be easy.

The state also already provides merit goods, those goods which society has determined to be so meritorious that they should be available to everyone for free or at minimal cost

It is suggested that government in capitalism should promote competition and the free-enterprise system when it is in conflict with the actual true purpose of capitalism to expand and further entrench the power of the capitalistic class irrespective of cost to others. This conflict with the capitalistic state is both as it has historically existed and as it is presently constituted.

Capitalism can be defended only if it is competitive. The degree of the slope of the demand curve of the profit-seeking firm must somehow be limited to some socially acceptable degree. Some economic activity is mundane and unobtrusive. In such cases even if not always socially beneficial, economic activity should be left alone. If the activity is other than mundane and unobtrusive, however, an active governmental role should at least be considered. Again, government involvement always presents risks and costs of its own, but it may be necessary anyway. No one ever said it would be easy.

In an individualistic society such as a capitalist one must be if it is to function anywhere near its theoretical potential, much social harm is caused by individual acts of self-interest. Individuals do not consider costs that do not affect them directly. As should be expected when most economic decisions are made by individual economic units operating in their own self-interests, those decisions will be made without regard for the interests of the economy as a whole. The result of this microeconomic decision making is macroeconomic problems.
Largely absent from the business decision-making process are ethical considerations. The resulting amoral or immoral decisions impose social costs. Unless those costs are made to be direct ones, firms will continue to ignore them. Only a more powerful

force, a government, can impose the empirical limiting operating conditions required to include elements previously excluded from it. The capitalist produces where marginal cost equals marginal revenue in order to maximize profit. Unless those external costs are included in the economic calculus, they will be ignored except by a very few.

These problems can be dealt with only at the macro level, so sometimes governmental intervention is required to limit individual activity for the benefit of all.

The capitalist argues that because property rights are inviolable even if negative externalities result from its use, it is the responsibility of those who want them stopped to bribe the property owners. If the bribe is larger than the benefit obtained by the property owner, the owner will cease producing the negative externality. This argument is balderdash. Property rights are not inviolable. They are a creation of the state, and the state has a right to limit them.

Inviolable property rights and unlimited individual license are not economic freedom. Economic freedom means that one is free to pursue their economic activities as they see fit, but within socially, politically, and legally established parameters. Individual license is a demand to avoid these parameters.

Economic freedom brings with it complementary responsibilities. The exercise of economic freedom conditions that enable one to exercise economic freedom in the first place. One such condition is an economic atmosphere of competition. In the current capitalistic society, it is not reasonable to expect individuals to consider the interests of the macroeconomy above their own. Governmental intervention is required.

Further because unlimited economic license is destructive of competition and because a free market cannot be said to truly exist without competition, unlimited individual license cannot be allowed if a society really desire a free market. Again, some kind of governmental involvement is required.

What is said here about the imperfections of capitalism must also be said about any system that might have the ability to control prices. Government action might be necessary if trade associations, resource cartels or labor unions practice noxious market control. Other sectors of the economy should not be allowed to hold already modified corporations hostage.

Even though unions arose and developed in response to problems imposed upon labor by profit-seeking capitalist firms, the activities of labor designed to counter those problems and impositions must also be limited if the problems and impositions are otherwise delimited. Hopefully, counter-activities will be less required in a modified corporate form.

Limitations should limit all parties' freedom to contract to being as equal as possible. Neither capital, irrespective of the mode of ownership, nor labor should hold the other hostage. It does not further social benefits. It reduces them.

It is recommended that there be more *competition* and a realistic extension of governmental activity. These changes would promote individual freedom at the expense of the firm's power just as advocated by capitalism's ideology. Unlimited individual license is not the same as economic freedom.

People need more than just material things and the leisure to enjoy them. Their nature has a need to participate. Not fulfilling this need produces alienation. An economic system must provide for a high degree of participation by everybody if it is to further the human condition. Worker participation in the production process would reduce alienation. The workers would choose production techniques, processes, firm sizes, etc. that would eliminate alienation. If alienation wasn't eliminated or reduced immediately, it would likely happen over time as the workers learned through the process of deciding. If they didn't eliminate or reduce alienation, a case could be made that they deserved to be alienated. Much alienation would now be the result of their actions, and who better should suffer negative results than the perpetrators of the actions that caused them?

The propaganda brought out against these proposals by the power-brokers would be so great that great political expertise would be needed to make them palatable to the electorate.

Capitalism's ideology maintains both that private property is inviolable and that government should not involve itself in the economy. Both claims are wrong. Indeed, the second asserts an impossibility. Society must remove conflicts both between the reality of capitalism and its ideology and between the various components of society.

It won't be easy, but if the proposals are feasible, then the plan can be discovered in the process of doing it. Changes are necessary They must a be reasonable. Knowing the solution ahead of time is not probable.

There is no doubt whose self-interests are affected by these proposals and that they will rebel against them. However, so would a large number of people whose self-interest would be served by them and who still would not support them. The ideology of any given society is a force to be reckoned with. It is often believed in spite of evidence to the contrary. Difficult political questions will arise.

Does this particular political economic system reasonably account for all the costs incurred in economic transactions? Is the economic calculus of this system as complete as it reasonably can be? There is nothing intrinsically wrong with cost-benefit analysis. Often, however, its result is either that all costs aren't considered or costs which can't be adequately measured are represented as having been adequately measured anyway. Because inadequate measurements are in number form can give them a pow er that they don't possess.

The criterion of economic growth is an important one. Producing an equal or greater amount of economic goods with either the same or a lesser amount of resources, particularly labor, is obviously a benefit if there aren't any other accompanying costs or if those who pay such costs decide that they are worth paying. Unfortunately, all too often what is called economic growth does not occur in this way. An analysis adequate to expose confusion is mandatory.

The superior system is the most efficient, but efficient means considering all the types of efficiency as well as the costs of having each. If a political economic system is not efficient in these ways, it cannot be considered an efficient system.

The material standard of living is also an important consideration. A humanist standard of living is even more so. There are hazards of numerically measuring that which does not lend itself to such measurement. It is necessary to have some idea of how to measure economic welfare. All costs must be considered. There are all sorts of subjective considerations, and what is and is not an adequate standard of economic life is open to interpretation. But within reason, economic analysts should know what is minimally reasonable relative to the claims made for a system.

How does the individual *qua* individual fare in a given political economy? If there is any justification whatsoever for the existence of the state, it is that it enables individuals to better their human condition and to develop into better individuals. Irrespective of the economic system, people will have rational self-interest. It needs to be allowed for but not pandered to. It should be developed into a constructive social force as opposed to a destructive one. There are many instances where the interest of the other is truly mine.

Does the political economic system meet an adequate minimum standard of distributional justice? If a society has the resources, "everyone has a legitimate claim on economic benefits to at least the minimum level necessary for the social protection of human dignity. . . . all persons really do have rights in the economic sphere." People are social beings, They grow in society. They cannot grow if they do not have the basic physical resources to participate in their society with dignity. "People have a right to work." They have a right to survive by their own efforts without interference from others. The opportunity to work is so important that a society that makes it difficult is a less-than-adequate society. No one ever said it would be easy.

Ed's <u>Hammering *Nails* Can be Murder,</u> <u>Felony Murder,</u> <u>Sometimes the Innocent Pay</u> , <u>The Droopy-Eyed Bank Robber</u> and <u>The Gringo Mayor of Ajijic</u> will all be published soon. An e-mail to me at <u>eddiegTHOI@gmail.com</u> will get you the info you need.

AVAILABLE NOW

Hammering *Nails* Can Be Murder

1   John-John

"Hey, Eddie G. Hey! It's about time! Where you been,? Where you been? I need to talk to you, Eddie G. I need to talk to you right now, Eddie G. Right now! It's important, Eddie G. It's important!"

Eddie G., that's me, that's what John-John calls me. To most of the others here at The Hyde Out Inn, a bar I own along with several other things here on the Southside of Chicago, I'm just Eddie. The *Eddie G.* is followed by a *longer-than-any-last-name-needs-to-be-spelled-with-almost-nothing-but-consonants-Polish-last-name-that's-mostly-unpronounceable-even-by-me.*

It was not quite noon and I was just getting to the bar. Downtown business had kept me busy until now. I had left word yesterday that I had things to do this morning and wouldn't get in until around lunch time, maybe even later. I guess word hadn't gotten around to John-John, or if it had, he was just too anxious about whatever it was with which he was concerned to let it interfere with the ants he had in his pants.

John-John is the janitor here at The Hyde Out Inn as well as my general *go-to-maintenance-guy.* More important, he is also my friend as well as my *lookee-after.* He wasn't retarded, but he surely wasn't quite normal. I would guess his IQ was about 90 or so, maybe a bit less. In addition to his squeaky voice, he has this habit of repeating himself a lot as well as using the *dive-bar* nickname of the person to whom he is speaking in almost every sentence. His habit sometimes rubbed off on me. When I spoke to him, I often did it as well.

Even at a distance and the unusually loud, for him, volume, I could see that his approach was hesitant, but he kept on coming. It was clear that he was excited about something. We came together far closer to the door through which I had just entered which hadn't even closed yet than to where he was originally standing when he first saw me. Besides his rushing towards me, it was also that his squeaky voice was a lot louder than his usual timid self that led me to the astute conclusion that it really was something important, at least important to him. With John-John, really important and important to him were sometimes far apart. No matter! Either way, it would be important to me. John-John was my friend.

He stopped just a few feet in front of me and repeated himself, this time in his more usual quiet voice."It's about time, Eddie G. It's about time! Where you been? Where you been? I need to talk to you, Eddie G. I need to talk to you right now, Eddie G. Right now! It's important, Eddie G. It's important!"

"Sure, John-John, go ahead. What's so important?"

"I know you are always there for me, Eddie G. I know you are always there for me. That's why I come to you, Eddie G. That's why I come to you. I want you to look at this, Eddie G. I want you to look at this."

He handed me a wrinkled article from the Hyde Park Weekly.

"While I was cleaning up yesterday, I found this old newspaper in the women's john, Eddie G. I found this old newspaper in the women's john. I put it in my back pocket to read later when I went to bed and had the television on. I always read better with the television on, Eddie G. I cut this article from the paper so I could show it to you, Eddie G. I cut this article from the paper."

The article was dated May 13, about three months ago. It was a *What Happened To?* type of article. A quick speed read told me it was about Samuel "Nails" Morton, a Chicago Jewish gangster, who died in a Lincoln Park horse riding accident on May 13, 1923, 45 years ago.

Then, he said, "I know I don't read all that good, Eddie G., but I was there when this happened. I was there when this happened. I don't remember much, but I know I was there. This man's last name was Morton, and my last name is Morton, John-

John Morton. What do you think about that, Eddie G? What do you think about that?"

Whatever this was about, it made my friend highly disturbed. I needed to help him if I could. I said "Wow, John-John. That's really interesting. Do you remember why you were there? Who you were with? Do you remember anything else?"

"I know I was there, Eddie G. I was with my nanny, Eddie G. I was there with my nanny. I heard a loud noise, like a gun shot. The horse jumped around, and the man fell off. The man fell off, Eddie G. And, the horse finally fell over and landed right on top of the man. The horse landed right on top of the man, Eddie G. I have been trying to remember more, but, that's all I can remember, Eddie G. That's all I can remember."

"You say you were with your nanny, John-John. What was your nanny's name?"

"My nanny's name was *nanny*, Eddie G. My nanny's name was *nanny*. Why are you asking me all these questions, Eddie G.? Why are you asking me all these questions? I want you to help me, Eddie G. I want you to help me. I want you to help me remember, Eddie G. I could hardly sleep last night thinking about this thing," he said pointing to the article. "I usually sleep good, Eddie G. I usually sleep good, but I didn't sleep good last night after I read this story. I work hard and I always sleep hard. I don't want to not remember and not sleep good. Don't you believe me, Eddie G? I remember this. I really do, Eddie G. I really do. Why don't you believe me, Eddie G.? Why don't you believe me? Charles would have believed me, Eddie G. I know Charles would have believed me. Why don't you believe me? Please help me, Eddie G. Please help me."

Charles had been an important man in both of our lives. Charles died three years ago today.

Even though I felt for John-John, I guess my questions were upsetting him more than he already was. His repeating himself had become even more intense than usual. I tried again, but more smoothly this time. I put my hand on his shoulder. I talk a lot, but I'm a *toucher* at heart.

"Yes, John-John, Charles would have believed you. And, I

believe you. But, I have to ask these questions so I understand what you're telling me. I have to get my ducks in a row."

"OK, Eddie G. Ask away. I'll help you get your ducks straight, Eddie G. I'll help you get your ducks straight."

My friend's dilemma confused me. After all, the thing upsetting him seemed to have happened over forty-five years ago. But still, I knew I needed to help him. That responsibility has always been part of my love for him. But, I needed to understand a lot more if I was going to be able to do so.

"Part of my problem is that I never knew you had a nanny. You were about five years old when this thing went down, right?"

"Yeah, I guess that's about right, Eddie G. I guess that's about right. I never remembered having a nanny either, until I read this story, Eddie G."

"Who else do you remember being there, John-John?"

"I don't remember nobody else being there, Eddie G., except the two policemen who came right after the horse landed on the guy."

Of course, I wanted to help him. I had to help him. John-John was my friend long before I inherited him from Charles as my employee and *lookee-after*. Besides that, I loved him. Just as Charles would have, so will I do anything possible to help him with his agitation. I didn't know yet what to do. Neither did I know yet what he wanted me to do. Hell, even if he knew what he wanted me to do, I didn't know if I could do it. I just knew I would try. Anyway, I asked him.

"John-John, what do you want me to do?"

"I want you to help me remember, Eddie G. I want you to help me remember."

"OK, John-John, I'll do my best to help you."

He still looked hanged dog. His finding this article was causing him an unusual despair in contrast to his normal happy self. I knew it was important for me to do something though I still didn't know what it could be.

"Be sure you don't forget, Eddie G. Be sure you don't forget. I really need you to help me, Eddie G. I really need you to help me."

"I won't forget. But, this thing happened over forty-five years ago. Right now, I don't even know where to start looking for answers. So remember, John-John. I want to help you. But, I don't know how to do it. You know I am as busy as a one-armed wallpaper hanger."

"A one-armed wallpaper hanger. That's funny, Eddie G. That's funny. But, I understand, Eddie G. I understand. Maybe, you won't help me, Eddie G. Maybe, you won't help me."

"Not won't, John-John. But, maybe I can't. This thing happened forty-five years ago. But, I promise you. I'm gonna try."

"OK, Eddie G. OK! Now, I gotta go eat, Eddie G. I gotta go eat. It's late for me. I have a lot of important work to do, Eddie G. I start my work early. I am hungry early. I have to eat before The Pickle gets too crowded, Eddie G. I have to eat before The Pickle gets too crowded. If I don't eat early, I lose a lot of time waiting for everybody else to eat. Then, I don't have enough time to do my important work, Eddie G. I don't have enough time to do my important work."

John-John wandered away to get his lunch.

I didn't yet know what to do or how to do it, but I knew I would try to do my best for him. I had to figure out what to do next. To do first, really. Tribune John would be in this afternoon as he was every afternoon. Maybe, he could get copies of the old original newspaper articles from his newspaper's morgue so I could get a better handle on this thing. Until then who knows?

In any case, John-John is a blessing. I sat down and reread the article, more slowly this time.

2   What Ever Happened To?
Hyde Park Weekly

Forty-five years ago today, the gangster, Samuel "Nails" Morton, died on a chilly Sunday afternoon. Nails was called *Nails* allegedly because of his *superior qualities* in gang fights. He was said to be *tough as Nails*. Nails went for a morning canter in

Lincoln Park just off of Clark Street near the statue of Benjamin Franklin when his nervous and meddlesome horse reared up and threw him. Morton landed on the grass with a thud. The horse landed a bit softer. The horse landed on top of Nails, hammering him in the head. The horse pounded. Morton died. That gave rise to the gruesome joke 'For the hammering of a horseshoe, Nails was lost.'

According to another story printed a few days later, a 'firing squad of morons,' composed of Morton's henchmen, returned to the stable. They rented the same horse that had hammered Morton, took the poor animal out to the same location in Lincoln Park and bumped it off in accordance with gangdom's code. They then sent a legendary message to the stable's owners: "We taught that *fucking* (*expletive deleted* in both this article and the original one) horse of yours a lesson. If you want the saddle, go and get it."

Morton was well known in Chicago. A year before the accident, the bootlegger gangster and a partner had both been acquitted in the killings of two Southside Chicago Police Detectives.

Morton's funeral was a spectacular one. As a World War I hero, the American Legion buried him with full military honors. As was always the case with gangster funerals, there were more flowers than one could count. Morton's alleged occupation was a florist, as was Dean O'Banion, his fellow gangster and friend, a real one. All the bad guys in all the gangs were there, including all the enemy gangs as well. That meant that the attendees included Johnny Torrio and Al Capone. Supposedly, 25000, *thousand*, not hundred, showed up.

It was a *helluva* funeral.